To Phyllis & Barney

Merry Christmas
&
lots of happy memories
from

Judy & Joe

VANPORT

SHIPS FOR VICTORY

VANPORT
MANLY MABEN

 OREGON HISTORICAL SOCIETY PRESS

The V-shaped eagle on the cover and title page
was found in "The Yard" section of The Bo's'n's Whistle,
a magazine put out by the Oregon Shipbuilding Corporation,
which was part of the Kaiser Company, Inc.

The production of this volume
was supported in part by
the Fred Meyer Charitable Trust.

This publication was designed and produced by
The Oregon Historical Society Press.

Library of Congress Cataloging-in-Publication Data

Maben, Manly.
   Vanport.

   Bibliography: p.
   Includes index.
   1. Vanport (Or.)—History. I. Title.
   F884.V36M33   1987   979.5'49   86-5184
ISBN 0-87595-118-X

90 89 88   4 3 2

Printed in the United States of America.

TO VERNICE

CONTENTS

VANPORT

FOREWORD

Most people who know of Vanport know of its death in the calamity of the 1948 Memorial Day flood, when at least 15 persons died as a result of the Columbia River's surging waters breaking through a railroad dike. This book, by contrast, is mainly about the life of Vanport, about its significance locally and nationally for the years of World War II and its immediate aftermath. Vanport was the largest wartime housing project in the United States and came, in many respects, to encapsulate the importance of the war to the economic and social development of the state of Oregon.

World War II had an enormous effect upon Oregonians. It rescued them from the economic doldrums of the 1930s by bringing new industries. It added to the diversity of the population. It increased the role of the federal government in the lives of citizens, and it disrupted family and community life. All of these changes were mirrored in Vanport.

Before American entry into the war, Oregon's major industry, forest products, was suffering from the lack of national and international markets due to worldwide underconsumption. The New Deal's National Recovery Administration—even before its demise at the hands of the Supreme Court in 1935—had done little to stabilize the industry. The state's second industry, agriculture, still suffered from falling income through most of the

decade, although New Deal farm programs had helped farmers to some extent. Similarly, tourism was destroyed by the Depression. Few Oregonians, let alone visitors from other regions, could afford to patronize Oregon's state and national parks. Throughout Oregon, economic distress led to labor-management conflicts, the most dramatic of which was Portland's bloody waterfront strike of 1934. There were strikes in the lumber industry as well.

Oregonians who participated in the colorful and calamitous events of the 1930s were almost all native-born Americans of Northern European Caucasian descent. They congratulated themselves on their Americanism. In spite of the troubles of the Depression, they took pride in their country, its institutions and its ideals. Most had taken hope from the New Deal, voting for Franklin Roosevelt in 1932, 1936, 1940 and 1944. But not even President Roosevelt's infectious optimism could completely clear away their lingering fears about the Depression and the rise of totalitarianism abroad.

Pearl Harbor swept away this sense of national malaise. It solidified the country in the face of an obvious menace to democracy. It called forth a mighty reshaping of the national economy. President Roosevelt declared that the United States "must become the great arsenal of democracy." Oregon's economic contribution to the war effort was to produce ships, food, fiber, and aluminum. But a state small in population required an influx of workers to supplement its labor force in order to increase production.

Manly Maben's book, *Vanport*, records a central part of the story of Oregon's participation in World War II. Vanport began as a private housing project of Henry Kaiser. Kaiser needed to shelter the thousands of war workers who came to the Portland area to work in the three major yards of his Oregon Shipbuilding Corporation. Vanport soon became the responsibility of the federal government through its local office of the Federal Public Housing Authority, the Housing Authority of Portland. Vanport's citizens participated in several unique experiences which are told for the first time in this book in a comprehensive manner.

Vanporters were one of the few groups of American civilian citizens who had no elected, municipal government whatsoever. Only late in the project's history did they participate at all in civic affairs. Vanport held the first large urban non-white population in Portland's (and Oregon's) history. The black population of Portland in 1940 was 2,565; in 1944 Vanport's black residents alone numbered around 6,000 and a 1946 estimate put the total black population in the Portland area at 15,000. The arrival of a substantial number of black immigrants posed problems for older Portland residents of both races. Racial segregation occurred in some areas of Vanport life: both black and inter-racial groups assailed it with some success. In the end, in spite of prejudice and the destructive flood, many Vanport blacks remained to contribute to the Portland community in the better days for race relations that lay ahead.

Regardless of race, Vanport residents confronted educational and family problems that were to become a part of the postwar American experience. Women as well as men worked in the shipyards. Since workers labored around the clock, new social services had to be created. Public schools added year-round terms, nursery schools and extended day care programs. Juvenile delinquency was a serious problem in Vanport. A high rate of adult crime was also attributed to the Vanport community, perhaps erroneously, by old Portland residents. After the war, Portland State University, one of Oregon's major universities—and the only urban one—grew from its beginning as the Vanport Extension Center of the Oregon State System of Higher Education, which was established for returning war veterans. It is perhaps fitting that the University, beleaguered throughout its history, was founded in the storm and stress of Vanport.

Manly Maben tells the story of Vanport objectively and sympathetically. He relates the larger dimension of its history—its regional and national importance—without neglecting the personal experience of men and women of humble origin. In the face of adversity, these ordinary people made a notable contribution to the war effort and to the history of the Pacific Northwest.

Through his meticulous scholarship, historical imagination and lucid prose, Manly Maben has given Vanporters their due. His book is a substantial addition to the historical literature of the Pacific Northwest.

Gordon B. Dodds
Professor of History
Portland State University

PREFACE

After approximately 30 years of teaching United States history in public high schools I decided to take a sabbatical leave and enjoy myself in some further study of the subject. A secondary benefit would eventually accrue; a little larger salary for the additional academic hours. I could live at home and commute to Portland State University, so I was on my way. It had been necessary to enroll in an advanced degree program, although I felt no compelling need in this regard. I concentrated on the histories of Twentieth Century United States and the Pacific Northwest under the tutelage of professors Jim Heath and Gordon Dodds.

As the time approached to select a thesis topic, Professor Dodds suggested a history of Vanport, Oregon; a scholarly work on the whole subject had never been done. The idea immediately touched a responsive chord.

I had come to the Portland area in 1940 as a fresh-out-of-college history teacher in Vancouver, Washington, and was here during Vanport's whole history. On Memorial Day, 1948, the day of the flood that destroyed Vanport, I was sitting in my car at a drive-in restaurant just across the Columbia River from Vancouver wondering where all the traffic on the Interstate Bridge was coming from. I got back over the bridge shortly before it was closed, avoiding an almost 100-mile detour.

After some digging, I discovered the Housing Authority of Portland (HAP) records were still in existence, although jumbled together in a janitorial storeroom at one of the then newer projects. These records, uncensored and in reasonable order, conscientiously compiled by the director, Harry Freeman, made the study possible. Besides the letters and miscellany of daily operations, there were the complete minutes of HAP Board of Commissioners' meetings, extensive newspaper scrapbooks, and related reports and publications of HAP, the Vanport Public Schools, and Vanport Extension Center (the precursor to Portland State University).

I began to realize that here, before the records vanished, was a chance to make a little contribution to the history Muse, Clio—a personal repayment of an unacknowledged debt (accumulated over the years) to my outstanding history professors who gave so much of their time, talent, and scholarship. I became deeply involved and utilized all my time in writing and research.

Many sources were used. Newspaper articles available at Portland State University and the Multnomah County Library were consulted only when necessary to supplement information established by HAP records, except in areas where these records did not exist, such as the planning and building of Vanport and the flood damage suits. Material from articles in national publications usually was too superficial for scholarly use, but did illustrate national attitudes. However, there are outstanding exceptions. *Architectural Forum* magazine provided excellent information on Vanport's design and layout, and judged their effectiveness, while the *American Sociological Review* contributed what might be termed the one scholarly study, tenant instability in Vanport. Stanley Elkins and Eric McKitrick's articles in the *Political Science Quarterly* provided a yardstick by which to measure democratic participation. Miscellaneous sources were: personal interviews, some of which were taped; correspondence; the Oregon Historical Society collection of Martin T. Pratt papers; and finally, pictorial and map material was obtained from the Kaiser Memorial Library and the Oregon Historical Society. More map and pictorial information was available at the Multnomah County Library.

The thesis was finished. Along the way it had become a book-length history that attempts to interpret all the major facets of Vanport's history. The study was largely completed over a two-year period. I had hoped that the manuscript would be made available at Portland State University and perhaps, the Oregon Historical Society. However, Professor Dodds suggested to Bruce Taylor Hamilton (Assistant Director—Publications of the Oregon Historical Society Press) that he might look at it and determine if it should be published. Which he did, and here it is.

I received the help and assistance of many people. Cooperative HAP officials provided unlimited access to the records and a work area. Ard Pratt (chief of police, Vanport) gave frank, written answers to my queries. Harry Jaeger (Vanport city manager) and Lamar Tooze (member of the board of commissioners, HAP) consented to taped interviews. Others responded, whether able to provide the desired information or not. Professor Jim Heath read the manuscript and offered helpful criticism and suggestions. With the guidance of the above-mentioned Mr. Hamilton, the staff of the Oregon Historical Society Press (Tom Booth, Adair Law, Lori McEldowney, George Resch, and Krisell Steingraber) helped to bring the book together in its final form.

Finally, and most importantly: Professor Gordon Dodds, who from beginning to end advised, counseled, made suggestions and spent much time above and beyond the call of duty; and my wife Vernice, who, with only high school typing, did each succeeding manuscript, while learning the intricacies of footnoting. I thank them all.

VANPORT

THE NEED, THE IDEA, THE REALIZATION

Vanport City's history was short but meteoric. During the early part of World War II, this city, the largest housing project in the United States and probably in the world, was conceived, designed and completed in the space of one year's time. Five-and-a-half years later it was dead. Located on the floodplain of the Oregon side of the Columbia River between Vancouver, Washington and Portland, Oregon, the city was reclaimed by the river on Memorial Day, 1948. Vanport, and the shipbuilding program out of which it grew, attracted national attention to the Portland area on a scale unrivaled since the 1905 Lewis and Clark Exposition. At least 39 articles about Vanport appeared in national magazines, including both the mass circulation periodicals and the technical journals.

Portland had become, in early 1942, one of the few major shipbuilding centers in the United States. In addition to the small, previously existing local yards, Henry Kaiser had built or was in the process of constructing three huge shipyards: "Oregon Shipbuilding Corporation," near the St. Johns Bridge over the Willamette River; Swan Island, upriver toward downtown Portland; and the Vancouver, Washington yard, situated a short distance above the Interstate 5 Columbia River Bridge. Swan Island built tankers, the other two the famous Liberty ships. Oregon Shipbuilding launched the area's first Liberty on 27 September 1941.[1] With United States entry into the war, the federal government made a gargantuan effort to increase ship production, and Oregon Ship quickly became the nation's leader in the production of Liberty ships. In August 1942, nine ships were completed, and construction time averaged 50.2 days per ship. It was predicted that by September completion time could be lowered to 40 days, and that ships could be produced simultaneously on every one of the 11 ways.[2] By the end of September 1942, a year after the first Liberty's launching, 76 additional ships had been completed and a national record established with the *Joseph N. Teal*, which was built in a few minutes under 14 days. President Franklin D. Roosevelt was present for the launching of the *Teal*, although his presence was not revealed for several days because of voluntary press censorship.[3] Oregon Ship typified the performance that had prompted Winston Churchill's remark, on 27 September 1942, that the American shipbuilding record was "almost unbelievable."[4]

One of many ships launched from the Kaiser shipyards. Notice the boats on the other ways in various stages of construction. (OHS neg. 68779)

1

The record breaking Liberty ship *Joseph N. Teal* was built in a few minutes under 14 days in September 1942. In August 1942 ship construction took an average of 40.2 days. (OHS neg. 68765)

At the end of 1942 Oregon Shipbuilding Corporation still maintained its production lead. At the same time employment in the three Kaiser yards reached almost 75,000, and was expected shortly to climb to 100,000.[5] Before the war, Portland had been an area of light industry, with a population of about 340,000 people, but within a year following the declaration of war the region had added approximately 160,000 new workers.[6] Gathering this work force became a major problem. On 20 September 1942, the Kaiser Company, in a full-page advertisement in the Portland *Oregonian*, appealed for 10,000 more workers—"no experience necessary." It exhorted people in the name of patriotism, and also pointed out the practical advantages of shipyard employment by printing the high wage scales.[7] However, a local work force of the necessary magnitude simply did not exist, and widespread outside recruiting took place. Perhaps the outstanding example of this effort was the Kaiser Company's attempt to recruit 20,000 workers in New York City. Somewhat typical was the case of the New York butcher who signed with Kaiser, closed his small shop, traveled to Portland, quickly obtained an advance in pay, and was soon sending money home in order that his wife and children could come as soon as he found a place for them to live.[8]

Recruits were obtained faster than transportation could be arranged in spite of the necessity for United States Employment Service approval. A great deal of publicity was given to the first 17-car train, dubbed the Kaiser Special, which arrived in Portland from New

New recruits to the Kaiser shipyards packed up their belongings and came from all over the country to help with the war effort. This car was parked outside the unfinished Vanport City housing project. (OHS neg. CN 007034)

November 26, 1942   Vol. 2, No. 22

The
BOSN'S WHISTLE

FOR OUR LIBERTY
WE GIVE THANKS

OREGON SHIPBUILDING CORPORATION · KAISER COMPANY, INC., VANCOUVER AND PORTLAND

Cover photo from *The Bo's'n's Whistle*, the weekly magazine of the Kaiser shipyard. (*The Bo's'n's Whistle*, 26 November 1942)

York. By mid-November 1942, 2,500 workers (including about 300 blacks) had been brought to Portland, mostly in special trains.[9] Family groups came from many areas of the nation, with the John H. Braukmiller family perhaps constituting the numerical record; 25 members came in successive stages from Iowa, 15 of whom worked simultaneously on the graveyard shift at Kaiser's Swan Island yard, including father, eight sons, one daughter, one son-in-law and four daughters-in-law.[10]

The importation of blacks, a group that played an important role in the Vanport story, caused some ripples in the placid calm of Oregon's almost non-existent race problems. Because of the automatic deduction of union dues by employers, forced integration of the local unions began to occur. However, the Kaiser Company agreed to drop the New York hiring when the American Federation of Labor (AFL) unions, with closed shop contracts, agreed to supply the necessary workers. The unions felt the agreement pointed the way toward the solution of all the issues "including the troublesome Negro worker problem."[11]

The frenetic shipbuilding activity created a housing shortage of crisis proportions, necessitating the use of every stopgap measure while longer range solutions were in progress. A full-page advertisement placed in the *Oregonian* by the Kaiser Company sketched the desperate situation and appealed for help in the name of patriotism. Thousands of housing applications were on file. Five hundred people had slept in their cars the previous night. Emphasis was placed on a recent Office of Price Administration ruling permitting immediate eviction and other tenant regulations. The advertisement

17 September 1942 Portland *Oregonian* advertisement.

3

20 Sept. 1942 Portland *Oregonian* advertisement showing the wage scale in the Kaiser shipyards.

acknowledged some local prejudice by describing shipyard workers as ordinary Americans, "clean, indus-
trious—good folks to know and to help." It requested
anyone who had or knew of anyone who had any accommodations to please call one of the three Kaiser
offices or fill-in and mail a coupon included in the
advertisement. Types of accommodations desired included houses for sale or rent (furnished or unfur-
nished), rooms for single men or women, and store
buildings or other property that, with minor remodeling, could serve as living quarters. The Kaiser Company served as a clearing house in bringing together
buyers, realtors, renters, and landlords.[12] It even planned
on leasing the Portland Elks Temple as temporary housing for workers arriving on the third train from New
York City, but the train was delayed and other plans
were made.[13]

The recruiting caused some apprehension among
Portland's citizens. City Commissioner William A.
Bowes commented that if 20,000 migrants arrived be-
fore January 1943, they would be sleeping in the streets.
In late September 1942, C.M. Gartrell, chairman of the
Housing Authority of Portland (HAP) had stated that it
would be impossible to provide additional housing in

less than two months, even if approved by Washington immediately.[14] The assistant general manager of Oregon Shipbuilding Corporation, Albert Bauer, tried to reassure HAP officials, telling them that the Kaiser Company had plans for additional housing, but in the interim tents were being pitched on stream banks and some were being rented at trailer parks and other sites.[15]

Inadequate housing caused many people to spend most of their non-working hours in the streets. One author described Portland as "one huge dormitory for shipyard workers," with its streets jammed day and night. Restaurants appealed to people to eat at home.[16]

By September 1942, some theaters were running full-length shows starting as late as 2:15 A.M., with the box office open until 3 A.M. As late as mid-January 1943, plans to alleviate conditions were still being developed by the National Housing Authority (NHA), which suggested, in addition to home conversion into rental quarters and sleeping rooms, something called the out-migration plan. The *Oregonian* made an appeal to pensioners and others not working in "essential activities" to leave the area and go to places like Pullman, Washington or La Grande and Enterprise in Oregon.[17] Clearly, although Oregon Shipbuilding Corporation had

Henry Kaiser and his sons ushering Mrs. Eleanor Roosevelt around the Kaiser Vancouver shipyard prior to the launching of the aircraft carrier escort *Alazon Bay* in April 1943. From the left—Henry J. Kaiser, Mrs. Roosevelt, Edgar F. Kaiser and Henry J. Kaiser Jr. (OHS neg. 69465)

Aerial view of Vancouver Shipyard. Notice Mt. St. Helens in the background. (OHS neg. 68774)

launched its first Liberty ship more than two months before Pearl Harbor, the massive expansion of the shipbuilding industry and resulting influx of workers was not anticipated, and no adequate housing plans were made.[18]

But with United States entry in the war, Henry J. Kaiser quickly realized that a vast step-up in ship production would be hindered by lack of housing for the imported workers. He bought approximately 650 acres of slough, pasture, and truck farm land along the Oregon side of the Columbia River, planning what would be described as the "most spectacular of all" wartime housing projects and the major project of the largest local housing authority in the nation.[19] High dikes surrounded the newly purchased area on all sides. Forming the eastern dike was Denver Avenue, a link in the

6

Mrs. Victor Rick, wife of a shipyard worker, enjoys a day in a trailer camp in Vanport prior to the completion of housing units. Notice the small "Victory" gardens.
(OHS neg. CN 013484)

Seattle-Los Angeles highway; Swift Boulevard lay at the base of the main Columbia River dike; while on the west was the railroad fill; and finally from the south a dike blocked a backwater called Columbia Slough. By mid-February 1942, statements from Edgar Kaiser's office (in charge of the Portland area operations) specified the need for 10,000 more homes within walking distance of Oregon Shipbuilding Corporation, and denounced current HAP proposals as inadequate.[20]

Funds for wartime housing projects generally came out of Lanham Act appropriations funneled through the NHA and its subsidiary, the Federal Public Housing Administration (FPHA). But these monies had been expended, so Henry J. Kaiser went to the United States Maritime Commission with his plan. The commission authorized his proposed land acquisition and told Kaiser to proceed with its development, advancing the money (which it would get back when additional Lanham Act funds became available). Arrangements were made with FPHA to finance and administer the project, but the Kaiser Company was to build it, a deviation from the usual procedure of unilateral FPHA control. Edgar Kaiser then signed a cost-plus-$2.00 contract with the U.S. Maritime Commission for the $26,000,000 construction job, and Kaiserville (eventually Vanport City) was born.[21]

To draw the plans, the Kaiser Company selected the Portland architectural firm of Wolff and Phillips, designers of the Kaiser shipyards. In the summer of 1942, with the plans near completion, Senator Charles L. McNary announced the construction of a housing project on a site as yet unnamed but within a long walk of Kaiser's Oregon Ship and Vancouver yards. With two different government agencies and the Kaiser Company involved in design and construction decisions, Vanport differed from other wartime housing projects. In a letter to the Portland Chamber of Commerce replying to criti-

Aerial view of the land that became Vanport. This photo was taken in 1940. (OHS neg. 68811)

cisms of the project, HAP Executive Director Harry Freeman stated that only site planning and ground layout were left to local architects and engineers.[22]

Design objectives included the housing of as many people as possible with the least possible amount of building materials, particularly those designated as "critical." Even though the city was not expected to be permanent, J.W. Moscowitz, a nationally known city planner from New York, served as a consultant on the project's design. The Kaiser Company remained in charge of the architectural planning, but the design required FPHA approval, and there were many disputes. Kaiser Company was responsible for the inclusion of nursery schools and the numerous bus shelters scattered throughout the project. It demanded and obtained adequate landscaping over the protests of HAP, whose commissioners perhaps thought it a waste of money due to the project's temporary wartime purposes and also per-

Henry J. Kaiser (OHS neg. 69459)

C. M. Gartrell was the first Chairman of the Board of Commissioners for the Housing Authority of Portland. He served as chairman throughout the war. (OHS neg. 69468)

haps were offended by the complete bypassing of their organization. Certainly the Kaiser Company was much more aware of the relationship of adequate housing and community services to successful war production than either HAP or FPHA. One of the most significant disputes with FPHA centered on Kaiser's insistence that the community have its own fire-fighting equipment instead of relying on that of the shipyards three miles away. For-

9

tunately the Kaiser view prevailed, in light of the numerous fires that later occurred.[23]

The Housing Authority of Portland, which eventually would administer the project, had been created in December of 1941, through a Portland City Council resolution. Mayor Earl Riley quickly named its members, appointing C.M. Gartrell, a Portland bank official, chairman. Construction of Vanport (then known as the Denver Avenue Project) hardly had started before HAP voiced its objections. Gartrell contended (at a meeting on 21 September 1942) that HAP was being deprived of its authority; that in order to take care of the Kaiser Company the government was overlooking other Portland war industries. He maintained that Washington, D.C. had held up HAP's other requests, but as soon as the Maritime Commission got into the act, it had responded immediately and given the Kaiser Company everything it wanted. The Housing Authority of Portland was losing all control, Gartrell declared, and its members had to read the newspapers to find out what was

happening. He argued that if HAP had the $20,000,000 for the Denver Avenue Project it could have done a much better job, avoiding the congestion, police, health and fire problems that were going to arise.[24]

A few months later Gartrell elaborated on his objections in a speech to the Portland Realty Board. He claimed that the units could have been constructed where there were existing streets, sewers, water and electric lines. Thus existing stores, theaters, recreation centers, schools and parks could have been utilized. No land would have to be drained or additional highway construction done on a militarily important road.[25]

On 1 August 1942, FPHA approved the Kaiser Company's action in locating and purchasing a site, and on 18 August approved the site itself. The company then awarded the contracts. Prime general subcontractors were the George H. Buckler Company and Segman and Son, both of Portland; each would build approximately one-half of the apartment buildings and divide construction of the utilities, roads, special and public service

A view of the initial stages of construction on the Denver Ave. Housing Project (Vanport). This photo was taken on 7 October 1942. (OHS neg. 68819)

Skeletons of the future Vanport units. (OHS neg. 71106)

buildings of this "super-project." The Kaiser Company built the Denver Avenue underpass itself. The U.S. Maritime Commission remained technically in charge under a shipyard facilities contract until FPHA could provide the money. On 20 August, two days after the site approval, construction shacks and earth moving equipment appeared. Preliminary work on the one-and-a-half by three-quarter mile site, one-sixth of the area in sloughs, lakes and swamps, began on 21 August, and the first apartment buildings were started on 12 September, although the official order to proceed was dated 14 September.[26] Much of the specialized work, such as electric, sheet metal, painting, plumbing, and heating was sub-contracted. Albert A. Pierson, chief construction engineer for FPHA, was transferred from Arizona to supervise all construction. The original plans called for 6,022 units, but work on the project was only three days old when FPHA allocated 3,900 more to the Kaiser Company. Eventually 20 more units were added. Wolff

and Phillips were again employed to draw the additional plans, along with those of another elementary school and two more commercial centers. The plans now included, beyond those described above, three fire halls, 16 playgrounds, 19 miles of surfaced streets, a sewage and water system, an administration building with offices and recreation rooms, a library, a nursery, and a clinic. Initial scheduling called for the first apartments to be ready about 1 November, and all construction to be completed by 15 February 1943, which did not happen.[27]

By mid-October 1942, more than 2,000 workers were employed at the site, now dubbed "Kaiserville" (13,000 men and women were hired before its completion with a maximum of about 5,000 working at any one time). Labor recruiters were sent as far as Coeur D'Alene, Idaho. Heavy rains began. The project became a sea of mud with every month's rainfall above average (November's total was 14.39 inches). Snow lay on the ground for most of the last two weeks of January; 15.5 inches fell on 21 January. Women proved they could work successfully in the heavy mud, on jobs previously thought "too tough," such as ditch digging. In January 1943 one-third of the 3,000 construction workers were women.[28]

Prefab and production line techniques were utilized. A framing yard cut everything to size for the standardized buildings and did considerable prefabrication. Much waste was eliminated, and the division of labor lessened the need for so many skilled carpenters. All plumbing pipe was pre-cut and threaded. During the wet weather prefabricated material was hauled by caterpillar tractors pulling sleds. Throughout January the completed buildings were isolated in swampy mud, even though they were now occupied by approximately 6,000 people.[29] Because the buildings were deemed temporary they were not only constructed of wood, but were set on wood foundations, which, fortunately, enabled them to float like corks during the later flood.

The war effort encounters mud. An unusually wet winter plagued construction on Vanport. (OHS neg. 78869)

Construction of Nursery #1, 8 April 1943. Notice the completed apartment buildings in the background. (OHS neg. 68817)

Architectural Forum magazine had established criteria for wartime housing dealing with the conservation of materials and manpower, speed of construction, location within walking distance of places of employment, minimum health and safety standards, and facilitating the entry of women into war industry. The magazine felt that Vanport's shortcomings as a permanent city (lack of variety in the dwelling units, absence of a city center, casually scattered facilities and high density) were not relevant in an appraisal of wartime housing. It stated that Vanport City met its criteria as well as anything yet built and provided a much less monotonous appearance than most other wartime housing projects. Its schools were "well planned," "conform with advanced practice," and were located on adequate sites. The design standards were "well above those of the average housing project." [30]

The final architectural result was a patterned arrangement of two-story buildings 38 by 108 feet. Each building contained 14 apartments, and every four of them were linked to a central utility building by covered passageway. There were two other types of apartment buildings, but they were negligible in number (17 in all). The overwhelmingly prevalent structure resembled a two-story box, flanked by a parallel ground floor wing on each end. The apartments ran from front to back with a living room/kitchen area in front, then bathroom with a shower stall, a closet, and the bedroom in the rear. If the bedroom was closed off, the next apartment became a two-bedroom unit. There were eight of these on the lower floor and six on the upper. The utility buildings contained coal furnaces with their automatic hoppers, hot water tanks, laundry rooms, and rooms with bathtubs. One unusual architectural feature that attracted national attention was the fixed window, ventilation being provided by louvers below. This saved critically short hardware but sometimes caused panic, as when, during a fire, one tenant jumped through a window (fortunately escaping injury). [31]

Neither the city of Portland, Multnomah County, nor the state of Oregon was consulted on any phase of Vanport's planning. [32]

Major problems during the project's first months included traffic jams, priority difficulties and other wartime restrictions, shortages of skilled labor and materials, and labor problems. A traffic bottleneck developed

The view from Denver Ave. during the last stages of construction, 3 June 1943. The roads were eventually paved. (OHS neg. 35481)

at the juncture of Swift Boulevard, Denver Avenue and Union Avenue south of the Interstate Bridge. On 18 March 1943, the state highway commission awarded the bid for a huge traffic interchange, which would prove invaluable long after Vanport was gone.[33]

A major union jurisdictional dispute slowed construction most drastically, putting it behind schedule at least 60 days, according to HAP Chairman C.M. Gartrell. The AFL had picketed another area project in which CIO (Congress of Industrial Organizations) workers were being used so the CIO retaliated by picketing construction at Kaiserville. As a result CIO lumber mills cut off their deliveries, and AFL mills could not provide an adequate supply. The Congress of Industrial Organizations proposed that both sides withdraw and turn the

dispute over to negotiators in Washington, D.C., but the AFL refused. Eventually HAP referred the dispute to FPHA, whose senior labor relations advisor came to Portland on an appeal from the associated general contractors. This was not viewed very optimistically by the *Oregonian*, which declared in an editorial that the public knows the federal government is "chicken."[34]

In mid-February, building activity reached its peak, with the largest number of units under simultaneous construction. The last of Vanport's 9,942 buildings was completed and furnished on 12 August 1943, although it was 1 September before the official delivery and acceptance documents were completed, and 26 September before the prime subcontractor declared all work finished. The federal government owned everything in

14

the project except the high-voltage wire, transformers, and equipment for the very few wartime-approved telephones.[35]

Thirty tons of grass seed and 68,000 shrubs were planted under the supervision of Portland landscape architects.[36] As with almost all materials, there was a shortage of plants and shrubs, and many had to be imported from the Midwest. A somewhat uniform planting plan for each apartment building included shrubs, lawn, and 12 different flowers. The same optimistic view prevailed in regard to landscaping as with other aspects of Vanport. "Barren Grounds Giving Way to Beauty at Vanport City" was the Oregon *Journal* head-

line for a story describing the plans for the main entrance as a forthcoming oasis of beauty.[37] Thus, Vanport City was complete; people were living in it and ships were being built rapidly. Although an HAP residents' handbook would later describe it as being constructed of "material that will not stand up unless you take care of it," *Architectural Forum* now called it a "miraculous job."[38]

On 18 May 1943 dedication of the first recreation building (which was almost 100 yards long) served as the occasion for a semi-official opening for Vanport City some three months before it was finished. Local dignitaries and HAP officials watched as Philip H. Par-

The muddy conditions shown were typical of the entire construction period for Vanport. (OHS neg. 37471)

Paving the roads in Vanport. (OHS neg. 68800)

rish of the *Oregonian* introduced screen, stage, and radio star Gale Page to the more than 3,000 in attendance. Oregon's Governor Earl Snell sent a message. Radio station KALE broadcast the festivities, while the Oregon *Journal* headed its preview article "Vanport City Story Fantastic."[39]

The 12 August opening of the New Vanport Theater provided the opportunity for a typical official completion celebration. Approximately 6,000 people attended the outdoor ceremonies in front of the movie house. Entertainment was furnished by the local radio stars of KGW. Abe Berkowitz's orchestra with pianist Glenn Shelley and accordionist Ralph Hamilton, together with singers and comedian Ron Salt, played favorites of the time such as "Fine and Dandy," "It Happened in Monterrey," "Alice Blue Gown" and "That Old Black Magic." Speakers were limited to one minute and tried to comply. Portland Mayor Earl Riley offered his city's facilities, benefits and friendship, while declaring that Portland was making an effort to establish its own "Good Neighbor Policy." County Commissioner Frank Shull welcomed the city into Multnomah County. Vanport's operation was formally placed in HAP hands.

Harry Freeman, HAP executive director and C.M. Gartrell, chairman of the board of commissioners, accepted the lease from F.M. Crutsinger, FPHA's regional director for Oregon, Idaho, Washington, Montana and Alaska. Crutsinger declared that Vanport City took "first place among the world's housing projects."[40]

Speakers lauded the $26,000,000 project, and paid tribute to its sturdy construction. Crutsinger praised the overcoming of physical and psychological construction difficulties, "which have seldom if ever been encountered in a building project." Perhaps, aside from difficulties in obtaining material, he was referring to the union problems and large-scale employment of women during construction. Massive amounts of reasonably scarce materials had been collected, including 54,000,000 board feet of lumber, 24,000,000 square feet of sheet rock, 6,000,000 square feet of plywood, 10,000,000 square feet of firtex, 30,000,000 gallons of paint, 37 tons of nails and 38,000 doors.[41]

Into the approximately 650 acres of buildings were compressed 703 apartment buildings and 17 multiple dwelling units—a total of 9,942 individual housing units—181 service annexes and 45 special public and

16

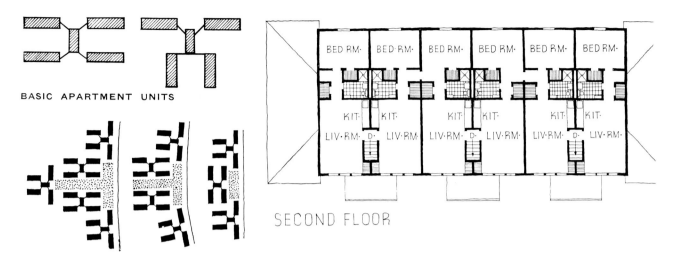

BASIC APARTMENT UNITS

TYPICAL SITE PATTERNS

SECOND FLOOR

A rendering of the basic apartment unit. (*Architectural Forum*, August 1943)

service buildings. These special buildings included an administration center, a U.S. post office, five grade schools, six nursery schools, three fire stations, a movie theater, five social buildings, a library, a 130-bed infirmary, a police station, 10 ice houses, six maintenance buildings and several commercial centers. Following the general completion ceremonies the New Vanport Theater held its own opening with all proceeds donated to the new Vanport Hospital. Patrons saw a double bill featuring Errol Flynn and Ann Sheridan in *The Edge of*

The finished apartment unit. (OHS neg. 78694)

Darkness and Alan Ladd, Helen Walker and Marie McDonald in *Lucky Jordan.*[42]

People already had begun to move in during the quagmire days of construction. The first group of units became available for occupancy on 12 December 1942, although occupancy was officially listed as beginning on 18 December. To be eligible, employment in a certified war industry was required, and of course shipyard workers comprised the vast majority of residents. The Housing Authority of Portland had to obtain special permission in January 1944 to set aside 15 apartments for the wives of servicemen being treated at Barnes Hospital in Vancouver, Washington. Approximately 400 families occupied the facilities by Christmas of 1942 and several hundred more came the following week. Coming from trailer camps, tourist cabins, rented rooms and hotels, they dodged workmen as they moved in. The Oregon *Journal* called it a "muddy miracle" and observed that the new residents were glad to be there, feeling that at least they were living in homes again.[43]

In mid-January 1943 Vanport's population reached an estimated 6,000 and by the end of March, 10,000. An HAP representative welcomed shipyard workers imported by the Kaiser Company who, if they had no funds, could get a wage advance in the form of a housing order. If necessary, money was also provided for pillows, sheets, and pillowcases, which were really the only necessities not supplied at Vanport. By the middle of June the project's population totaled more than half the expected maximum. In August the completed project was full except for about a thousand units that still lacked furniture. By early November HAP estimated occupancy at 39,000 using a family figure of 3.8 persons.[44]

Because of the impermanent nature of a sizable segment of Vanport's population, it was difficult to establish exact figures. The *Oregonian* fixed the maximum at 42,000. At any rate, the project was full and had a wait-

Old ice wagons reborn as ice houses. (*The Bo's'n's Whistle,* 26 November 1942)

ing list until the spring of 1944. People had been collected from points that spanned the country: New York City, the Blue Ridge Mountains, the Ozarks, the Sierras, and the Great Plains. Oregon naturally furnished

One of the 179 utility buildings containing laundries, janitors quarters, extra bathrooms, and central heating plants. (*The Bo's'n's Whistle,* 26 November 1942)

the most, but neighboring Washington could do no better than fourth; Minnesota was second, Texas third and Oklahoma fifth. By 31 March 1944, the only states not represented by families were Rhode Island, New Hampshire, Maine and Delaware. Not only was Vanport Oregon's second largest city, it rose to fifth place among Pacific Northwest urban centers.[45]

Two characteristics of Vanport's population quickly became apparent: residents were young, and they did not stay long. In August 1943 the average adult age was 33. The percentage of children under 10 was so high that the Oregon *Journal* called special attention to that fact. During 1944, with the war effort still intense, tenant turnover remained high. In September it was at 12 percent, almost double that of all other HAP projects. In much less than a year's time the turnover equaled the total number of units.[46]

The occupancy rate at Vanport City fluctuated wildly. It was unusual, like almost every aspect of life there. No sooner were requirements eased in 1944 than the Kaiser Company started an intensive new recruiting campaign, expecting to hire 12,000 more workers by November. The Housing Authority of Portland estimated that at least two-thirds of the occupants worked at the Oregon Shipbuilding yard. Restrictions were soon reimposed on all two- and three-bedroom units. Two men had been permitted to occupy a single-room apartment (women could have a single-room apartment all to themselves), but this was stopped in August. Again, for all practical purposes the project was full, with a waiting list for everything except one-room units.[47]

Occupancy reached its highest peak during January of 1945 (higher than the earlier full period because a smaller number of the units were in the process of renovation and cleaning). Then the shipyard layoffs started, with 3,000 being terminated the first week. A newspaper panic developed. On 7 February the Oregon *Jour-*

nal forecast a definite reduction in ship construction by summer; on 25 February the *Oregonian* printed a condensed *Fortune* magazine story predicting a slump for the booming West Coast cities; and the *Journal*, on 26 February, took pains to deny a rumor of impending layoffs at Kaiser's Vancouver yard. On 10 March Portland's *Daily Journal of Commerce* reported a Henry J. Kaiser speech in New York City, attributing to him the statement that Portland's yards would be closed by fall, with the Vancouver yards possibly operating into 1946. The *Oregonian* played down these really quite accurate remarks, pointing out that they were merely informal comments at a United Nations' clothing collection luncheon, transmitted to a Seattle newspaper by a New York correspondent. In early April the Swan Island yard

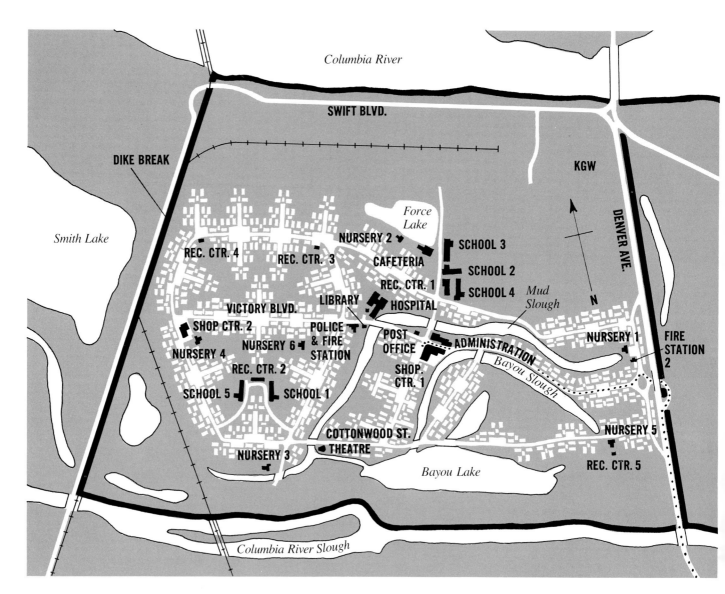

Columbia River

SWIFT BLVD.

DIKE BREAK

Smith Lake

KGW

DENVER AVE.

Force
Lake

NURSERY 2

REC. CTR. 4

REC. CTR. 3

CAFETERIA

SCHOOL 3

SCHOOL 2

REC. CTR. 1

SCHOOL 4

Mud
Slough

VICTORY BLVD.

LIBRARY

HOSPITAL

SHOP CTR. 2

POST
OFFICE

NURSERY 1

FIRE
STATION
2

NURSERY 4

POLICE
& FIRE
STATION

NURSERY 6

ADMINISTRATION

Bayou Slough

REC. CTR. 2

SHOP.
CTR. 1

SCHOOL 5

SCHOOL 1

COTTONWOOD ST.
THEATRE

NURSERY 5

NURSERY 3

Bayou Lake

REC. CTR. 5

N

Columbia River Slough

VANPORT

PUBLIC BUILDINGS

DIKE

RAILROAD

BUSLINE

went to one shift. Meanwhile, a large exodus from Vanport was underway. By June HAP was trying to obtain permission to give veterans a preference for housing, irrespective of occupation.[48] At the end of July the population at Vanport had dropped from the January high of approximately 40,000 to about 26,000.[49]

Another flurry of evacuations came with the sudden end of World War II. Portland newspapers reported tenants leaving in droves. The Housing Authority questioned this, reporting only 21 checkouts in a three-day period. However, it was busily checking on "skips," and the commissioners proposed contacting FPHA concerning rate reductions and permission for tenants to furnish their own coal with a corresponding rental re-duction. By September Harry Freeman freely admitted terminations had increased; 400 families moved out in a single week. Because of all the debris left by departing tenants, the garbage contractor was allowed to increase the fees charged to HAP. In November the exodus slowed with the project remaining slightly over half full.[50]

A Vanport Extension Center survey in July 1946, carried out with the cooperation of HAP, arrived at a population figure of slightly over 15,000, and forecast a drop to around 14,500 by January 1947. But as usual Vanport proved unpredictable. With eligibility requirements reduced, an influx of veterans, and the growth of Vanport Extension Center, the population grew to about 18,500 and stabilized there until the flood disaster.[51]

LIFE IN VANPORT

Life in Vanport possessed a hurdy-gurdy, kaleidoscopic, almost unreal quality, especially during the wartime years. Its 24-hour character, noise, 20-foot separation of apartment buildings, and sense of rootlessness all contributed to an atmosphere of vague disquietude so pervasive that two investigators of tenant instability concluded that it caused the illnesses (unrecognized by the tenants as psychic) that led many of them to leave the project. Perhaps it was this aspect of the city's life that elicited the most intense reactions and memories from Vanport's inhabitants. In spite of the fact that the literacy and expression level of Vanport's population was below average, these same investigators received an unexpectedly high response to their questionnaire sent to former residents during the winter of 1943–44; 55 percent of the respondents even appended additional remarks.[1]

Much of this under-the-surface impact was not apparent as tenants first moved into the green apartment buildings. Construction proceeded apace amid the mud of winter and the dust of spring and summer. Vanport became a city of the young, perhaps because the young are more adaptable and willing to change their environment. Neither military manpower demands nor the war's end ever resulted in much change in the age composition.[2] How this affected developments at Vanport City is difficult to assess, although it may have played some part in the absence of community spirit.

During the construction period residents experienced many inconveniences. Ice was to be delivered to the door, but for several months none was available. Until April 1943, no stores, grocery or otherwise, or cafeteria service operated. It was a one- to two-mile walk to Kenton in North Portland for supplies or for bus service to Portland or Vancouver. The commercial centers that opened in 1943 proved to be inadequate, and bids for three more were called for the following February. Shortages of butter and milk grew more severe in the project than in Portland's established communities, implying that suppliers took care of their old accounts first. The Kaiser Company demanded the milk products situation be remedied in order to retain workers, but the dairy industry replied that lack of a price incentive made this impossible. Streets in Vanport remained graveled until completion of construction, and so, after the winter rains, mud was replaced by dust.[3]

Postal service was inadequate, there was no grass, and the constant construction noise prevented swing and graveyard shift workers from sleeping. The nearest ration board, located at the intersection of North Interstate Avenue and North Portland Boulevard, quickly became swamped. A new board was finally created and

The kitchen area of one of Vanport's apartments, 17 December 1942. Mrs. Wilbur Simpson, one of Vanport's first residents, said that after a tourist camp, her two-room apartment was "wonderful." (OHS neg. 68823)

situated in Vanport City. By mid-July 1943, it served 26,000 people. Although it did not deal with fuel oil stamps or wood priorities (since Vanport furnished coal heat), and had little gas ration stamp business (most

Vanporters obtained stamps at the plants where they worked), a crowd big enough to fill the office quarters almost always collected before the doors opened.[4]

There were other problems. One gigantic traffic jam

Loading shipyard workers for a day's labor at Vanport. (OHS neg. 68821)

resulted from a mix-up over a trivial matter. The public utilities commission requested that state police check the "for hire" trucks crossing the Interstate Bridge. In the communications between the Oregon State police and Multnomah County Sheriff's Office this somehow was turned into a stop-all-autos-for-license check. A two-mile tie-up occurred on Denver Avenue and eight to nine thousand workers were an hour to an hour-and-a-half late for their shift at Kaiser's Vancouver yard, not exactly expediting war production. The very same day, a bridge opening for a tug pulling a log raft caused the swing shift to be late.[5] While construction was still in progress most Vanport residents probably tolerated what, it was hoped, were temporary inconveniences. Because of the severity of many of their previous housing problems many were glad simply to get into the newly finished apartments.

An apartment for two consisted of one room opening off the front of the building. In it was a "daveno" (also used as a bed), two occasional chairs and a dining table to seat four. Toward the back of the room was a cupboard with a sink and icebox below, and a double electric hot plate and small oven at one side of the sink. A small closet and a tiny bathroom with a shower were in the extreme rear. For larger families one or two bedrooms opened off the basic living room, furnished with a bed, dresser, and mirror. Actually, all essentials for living in the apartments were provided except pillows, linen, dishes, cooking utensils, and silverware.[6]

None of the windows opened save one in each of the upstairs apartments that served as a fire escape onto the porch roof. Most of the units contained no thermostat to regulate heat, and tenants who did have one were requested not to touch it, and to regulate the heat by closing the register rather than opening doors or louvers. At first there were no home telephones. In April 1944 the telephone company secured permission from the Housing Authority of Portland to use the light poles for phone wires, but the very few installed serviced only those persons able to get the difficult governmental authorization. A telephone exchange was not installed at Vanport until six months after the war ended. The utility buildings (one for each four apartment structures) had but two washing machines for 56 family units, while the original two shopping centers carried only a limited range of goods, and wartime restrictions made personal transportation difficult.[7]

Vanport's first tenants moved in amid much favorable publicity, anticipating pleasant conditions. However, it did not take long for dissatisfactions to grow, and ultimately the vast majority (administrators and tenants alike) agreed that Vanport was not a good place to live. As early as the winter of 1943–44 tenants were moving out at a rate of 100 per day (this later stabilized at about 35 per day).[8]

During the first year of operation, if not before, HAP realized that life in Vanport had its drawbacks. In late 1943, the John B. Pierce Foundation, located in New York City, planned a survey of wartime housing to determine the minimum space needed to carry on the basic functions of family living. The study had full approval of the War Production Board and the National Housing Administration. Because of the favorable national publicity Vanport City had received, the foundation selected it as one of the eight communities to be studied.[9]

The Housing Authority of Portland used every means at its command to quash the inclusion of Vanport City in the survey, and it was successful. Executive Director Harry Freeman, in his reply to the request, marshalled every possible argument to discourage the investigative organization: the Authority did not wish residents to be guinea pigs (even though only 100 families would be involved); people would react against the survey; the tenants were well adjusted and did not need surveying; there was a shortage of hotel accommodations for the investigators; travel conditions were bad; and HAP would be unable to furnish space. To this communication Freeman received a devastating reply delineating the survey techniques, listing objectives, reasons for the selection, and noting the cooperation the foundation was getting from everyone else. The survey team could manage its own housing and transportation needs. In case the team was welcome the courtesy of a wire reply was requested so preparations could proceed. Freeman, after discussing the request with Board of Directors Chairman C.M. Gartrell, refused it, citing the temporary, substandard nature of the project and the planned liquidation. He suggested that the survey be confined to permanent housing built by private enterprise, and that Seattle might be a good place to go.[10]

Charlotte Kilbourn and Margaret Lantis, who carried out a study that same winter, provide the best single source of information on resident dissatisfaction. They tabulated complaints about Vanport housing and the community in order of frequency (not necessarily in order of importance). Highest on the list for housing was the inadequate cookstove, followed by fear of fire, heating problems, mud, the cost of living, and other miscellaneous complaints. In regard to the community itself the complaint most often voiced was the presence of blacks and whites in the same neighborhood; then came (among others) inadequate shopping facilities, noise, troublesome children, the discriminatory attitude of Portlanders, and lack of segregation in the schools. The almost complete absence of community social organization received little mention; apparently most residents did not expect it.[11]

How much could be inferred from these responses is debatable, as it turned out that of the three main reasons tenants had given for leaving the project, two had no connection with the above complaints and the third was only slightly related. The main reason for moving out was the family head entering the armed forces, followed by job conditions and, third, illness in the family. Certainly the first reason applied equally to individuals moving from any community in the United States, especially if the young age composition of Vanport is considered. Another contemporary observer who noted the

A view from the front room through to the bedroom of a basic Vanport apartment units. (*The Bo's'n's Whistle*, 26 November 1942)

high job dissatisfaction in Pacific Coast shipyards in general and the Vancouver yard in particular, offered an explanation that today might seem strange. The cost-plus system, on top of poor organization, made it almost impossible for workers to keep busy. Those who had come to do a conscientious job in furtherance of the war effort were disillusioned. For illness to be a particularly significant reason it had to be brought on by conditions in Vanport. Kilbourn and Lantis considered it legitimate to assume that many people were unable to

Interior view of the front room through to the bedroom of a basic Vanport apartment. (*The Bo's'n's Whistle*, 26 November 1942)

adjust to the noisy, three-shift, individualistic, anonymous life, and gave illness as the reason for leaving. However, the fourth leading reason for leaving, heat, definitely was connected to project living conditions.[12]

Obviously, many dissatisfactions did develop, and

quickly. Another 1943 tenant survey contained the question, "Do you consider prices higher in Vanport?" Out of 194 responses to this question 174 replied yes, even though a December issue of *Business Week* observed that a contract lease provision that prices be kept close

Opening day of the grocery store in Commercial Building #1, 8 April 1943. (OHS neg. 68797)

to Portland's was being followed, and that HAP claimed many prices were lower than those in downtown Portland. However, by August, complaints of inferior food and higher prices in project stores did elicit comment from HAP commissioners.[13]

The sheer volume of noise was always a factor in Vanport. Only recently have scientists become aware of the insidious effects of high noise levels on human beings. The multi-occupancy dwellings, construction that allowed easy transmission of sound, around-the-clock life, cramped quarters (which encouraged sending children outside), and closeness of the buildings all contributed to an almost intolerable noise level. There were many complaints. By July 1944 the situation was so bad that Oregon Shipbuilding Corporation, believing it was affecting employees' work performance, sent a letter to HAP regarding the noise and other disturbances. During

the same month an irate Vanporter complained to radio station KEX. Executive Director Harry Freeman's only answer was that HAP could not exclude families with children, and that noise was difficult to control because Vanport had to operate as a "24-hour town."[14] Implied, of course, was that the noise would continue.

Many additional complaints referred to "partying" and drunken brawls, and the disturbances they created, making it impossible to get sufficient rest. Allowing two single men to occupy a one-room unit added to the noise. These conditions, although real, became exaggerated in the telling—as did stories of juvenile depredation. One former Montanan moving to the area wrote to Senator Burton K. Wheeler that although he could not obtain other housing he did not want to go to Vanport because he was concerned for his children's well-being. This eventually led to FPHA concern about

Vanport's safety for children. After the complainant received good housing somewhere else, however, he admitted he merely had been repeating gossip.[15]

Two of the chief causes of mounting tenant antipathy toward Vanport were heat problems and fear of fire. Residents often resorted to the use of the surface stove elements and ovens for heating purposes. Heat pouring out of the open oven melted the bakelite control knobs so frequently that a serious repair problem ensued. Electric heaters were added surreptitiously, causing the fuses to blow, whereupon tenants simply overfused or added pennies to the switchboxes. Finally HAP issued a bulletin stating that on 1 November 1946, it would begin an inspection of units, and confiscate and hold any appliances that could cause "excessive load" until the individual left the project. If a second inspection again discovered offending appliances the tenant could be evicted.[16]

Where wood buildings—each containing 14 units—were spaced 20 feet apart the fear of fire was well-founded. Moreover, the origin of a fire that could kill a tenant and his family, plus destroy cherished belongings, might easily be beyond an individual's control. During the last half of the first year of operation there were many small fires. In 43 cases HAP attempted to collect charges for damages from tenants deemed responsible but it met with little success, collecting on less than one-quarter of them. The winter of 1943–44 also saw many fires for which residents were not responsible. These occurred primarily in the service and utility buildings. Because of the War Production Board restrictions the fresh air intakes had been constructed of plywood and in many places passed within five-and-a-half inches of the white-hot sections of the furnaces. Other fires began when water heaters ignited the walls behind them. By 1 May 1945, a total of 217 fires had broken out in these buildings. Alterations were finally made during that year.[17]

The frequency of fires increasingly worried the Seattle FPHA office. Monetary loss and excessive fire

Meat cases at one of the Vanport markets. (OHS neg. 68789)

protection expenses, rather than possible loss of life, seemed to be its greatest concern. On 30 March 1944, a fire killed one person and severely burned another; fatalities would have been much higher except for the lucky coincidence of a night shift worker who, passing by, noticed evidence of the fire and roused the tenants.

By now the HAP board of commissioners recognized that people hesitated to live in Vanport because of the fire hazard.[18] Throughout the history of the project fire remained a serious problem. In early 1943, with 2,500 of the almost 10,000 units occupied, the Vanport Fire Department had received only two pieces of fire protection equipment. The Oregon *Journal* quipped that until the rest arrived the residents would have to trust to the Lord and help from the Portland Fire Department. Vanport citizens became even more apprehensive when, in December 1945, a series of arson blazes started with the destruction of Shopping Center Number 1 and did not halt until a young culprit was apprehended a month later. As late as the time of the flood, the school district was seeking funds to replace a school destroyed by fire.[19]

The compactness of the units increased the tensions and problems of daily life. During 1943 and early 1944, the first period of maximum occupancy, many residents requested larger quarters. Tenants were assigned housing with the absolute minimum of space. Thus, a couple drew a one-room unit, and if the partners worked different shifts, which was not unusual, it was relatively impossible for one to do any housework as the other had to sleep in the room at the same time.[20]

A rather powerful irritant at Vanport was the insect and rodent problem. Residents frequently complained they could not sleep because the bedbugs were so bad. An exterminating company was called so often that a regular schedule of charges was worked out, a roach or flea call being the cheapest, with a progressive increase through rats and mice, bedbugs, and finally, cyanide

fumigation of the whole unit. By July 1944 complaints of bedbugs averaged almost 900 a month and of cockroaches, over 1,500. Finally in 1945 HAP obtained satisfying results with a new fumigation procedure. A heavy DDT spray of eight apartments (one pint per apartment) yielded excellent results with no call-backs. Fortunately or unfortunately knowledge of the residual effects of the new pesticide was unknown.[21]

How much the host of HAP regulations on buildings and grounds (which will be considered in detail in chapter 3) affected the general dissatisfaction with life in Vanport remains debatable, and HAP was not always the real culprit. Much of the unpleasant appearance of the project must be attributed to the residents themselves. On one scale, 90 percent of the whites and 100 percent of the blacks were classified as lower-middle-class. Many of the women were working, HAP believed the black residents crowded many extra persons into their apartments, and there was a general indifference to taking care of such a temporary abode. By 1944 many of the apartment interiors appeared rather tawdry, and although for a time tools and paint were furnished by the management division to those tenants who wished to improve their quarters, the practice was stopped when one of the labor unions maintained that furnishing this material was in violation of their contract.[22]

Originally quite an effort had been made to beautify the exterior environment. Thousands of shrubs had been planted; there had been a slough improvement program, and slough banks were graded; trees that did not interfere with construction were saved; and 10 acres had been set aside for (admittedly small) tree-shaded parks. However, the project quickly acquired a "ratty" look. Seattle's FPHA office began receiving uncomplimentary reports about the project's appearance, and these quickly were relayed to HAP. Trash and debris were everywhere, along with broken windows. Half of the apartments had never been equipped with waste paper boxes, and the containers that existed were soon demolished. Whatever the reasons, Vanport's residents did not do much to maintain or improve the looks of the project, especially during the wartime years.[23]

Outside the residences, other factors made life in Vanport at times unpleasant or inconvenient. The mosquitoes apparently were aggressive, and although the city and county were supposed to carry out a spray program with in-lieu-of-tax funds, the commissioners (early in 1944) decided unanimously to get the job done for that year no matter what the cost. As late as 1946 only one cafe in the project met all the requirements of the Multnomah County Health Department. The commissioners continually received complaints from Vanport merchants that peddlers were "over-running Vanport City," indicating HAP licensing requirements were being widely disregarded. Two environmental features that perhaps were more favorable were the very small number of gas stations and the absolute absence of billboards.[24]

The psychological effect of living on the bottom of a relatively small area, diked on all sides to a height of 15 to 25 feet, was vaguely disturbing. It was almost impossible to get a view of the horizon from anywhere in Vanport, at least on the ground or in the lower level apartments, and it was even difficult from upper levels.

It is reasonably clear that most of the residents did not particularly enjoy life at Vanport, especially during the wartime years. This was also true, though to a lesser degree, following the war. Vacancies in Vanport were increasing in 1944 despite a general housing shortage. The Portland Chamber of Commerce Executive Committee sent a letter to HAP maintaining that unsatisfactory housing conditions at Vanport City were responsible for a heavy turnover and manpower loss in industry. In addition to many of the dissatisfactions previously noted, the letter cited inefficient refrigeration, jammed doors and windows, and discourteous personnel. Harry Freeman admitted the tenants were becoming "restless and testy."[25]

The distribution and type of Vanport's occupants changed in the postwar period. Welfare recipients were concentrated there; income-adjusted rents were adopted; large numbers of veterans moved into the area's only available housing (many as college students) and the proportion of black residents rose markedly. But it was still the same impermanent, concentrated project, only older. Its residents still regarded their stay there as temporary, although not as transitory as its wartime population did. Fewer women worked, and being cooped up in Vanport was particularly trying to them. To the very end, life in Vanport remained a unique, and for many, a distressing experience.

LANDLORD AND BIG BROTHER

Although the project lease for full operation and maintenance was not publicly presented to the Housing Authority of Portland until 12 August 1943, many of the details had been arranged even before the first occupants moved into Vanport in December 1942. In late September HAP approved a supplemental development contract with the federal government in which the United States Housing Authority agreed to purchase HAP bonds. A month later HAP approved the management lease, even though its final form was not completed until almost May. Also in late October the name Vanport City (a contraction of Vancouver and Portland) was selected, approved by the Seattle office of the Federal Public Housing Administration, and in early November officially adopted. It took some time for the appellation to catch on. The previous designation, Kaiserville, by which the project had become commonly known, was unacceptable, as a presidential order had forbidden the naming of housing projects after living persons. Finally, in February 1943 HAP suggested to the Portland newspapers that they cease using Kaiserville, and Executive Director Harry Freeman asked Superintendent James T. Hamilton not to use it in material he was writing about the forthcoming schools.[1]

Harry Duke Freeman, a native of Paducah, Kentucky, who was to guide HAP through its most colorful period, had originally visited Portland on survey assignment for a St. Louis-based city planning organization. After several more years in St. Louis he moved to Portland in 1935 as a planning engineer with the City Planning Commission. He had a strong academic background for this type of work, having graduated from the University of Illinois in city planning, landscape architecture, and landscape engineering. Upon creation of HAP he became its head on a part-time basis and on 1 October 1942 assumed full-time status.[2] He was a wise choice, for he quickly exhibited great administrative ability.

Freeman was given a free hand in selecting project personnel. J.L. Franzen was chosen city manager. Franzen had grown up in the Yakima, Washington area, had graduated from Washington State University as a civil engineer, and for the past 17 years had been city manager at Oregon City, Oregon. The Housing Authority of Portland requested the Oregon City Council to grant Franzen a year's leave of absence during which time he would be on loan to HAP, with an option for HAP to renew the arrangement each year until the war ended or the project was discontinued. Oregon City consented to this arrangement, on condition that he be available for consultation and officially keep his Oregon City position at one-half salary. A large staff was collected, in fact larger than that of the whole Multnomah County government. Throughout the process HAP officials

Executive Director of Vanport, Harry Duke Freeman guided Vanport through its brief but vital history. (*From Roses to Rivets*)

worked in cooperation with F.M. Crutsinger, FPHA regional director.[3]

Vanport City appeared to be one of the Pacific Northwest's major cities. Actually, however, it was not a city at all, nor was it simply a housing project, because most community services were provided. It was never incorporated. It most closely resembled the corporation company town of an earlier era. Only now the town operator was HAP, in cooperation with the United States government. There was no mayor, council, court, or any other aspect of city government. There were no taxes, nor was there a single homeowner. Community business and civic organizations were sparse; HAP either furnished community services or contracted their operation out to others—as in the cases of police protection, schools, and commercial facilities. So HAP ran a huge quasi-business-governmental operation with a potential income of almost four-and-one-third million dollars from apartment rentals and more from business rentals.[4]

A staff for this huge operation had to be assembled quickly in the face of war manpower shortages, which perhaps explains the high rate of tenant complaints regarding the arrogant attitude of administration employees. The irritation may simply have reflected a universal anti-bureaucracy sentiment, although one administrator explained that at Vanport the complaints dealt mainly with rent collection, where (because of a high incidence of "skips" and collection difficulties) the administration had to be hard nosed. Each housing project was run as a separate entity with its own complement of employees.[5] The Vanport project made HAP the nation's largest local housing authority.

The rent schedule adopted was: a one-room apartment, $7.00 per week; two rooms, $8.75; three rooms, $10.15; and four rooms, $11.55. Rent included furniture, appliances, electricity, heat, garbage disposal and cans, laundry facilities, water, hot water, lawn care, and all maintenance, even of the furniture. Originally, rents were paid weekly in advance or, if the tenant preferred, by the month. Later it became monthly only (at essentially the same rates), and if not paid by the fifth the collection department was notified. Housing Authority personnel were authorized to enter an apartment to contact its tenant; if they did the tenant could demand identification, a rather insignificant right compared to that of entry.[6]

33

J. L. Franzen, first city manager of Vanport. (OHS neg. 96469)

REGULATIONS

The Housing Authority of Portland, in a conscientious effort to protect and preserve the taxpayers' property, established a host of regulations. Their sheer number raised controversy over the desirability of living under these conditions. Actually, it is improbable that much attention was paid them, or that they were strictly enforced. There was to be: no altering, subletting, or even allowing someone else use of an apartment; no additional occupancy without notifying HAP; no furniture removal or commercial use; no gambling; no adjustment of the thermostat or placement of items on the porch roof; no outside aerials; no candles on Christmas trees; and no playing in the sloughs or lakes.[7]

The regulations seemed endless. If the ice pan was not emptied frequently, a water damage charge would be made. Repair of furniture by the tenant was prohibited; instead, the maintenance service should be notified, and the tenant would not be charged for any damage deemed due to normal use. Any furniture brought into the project was at the owner's risk, as HAP carried no insurance on personal belongings and assumed no legal responsibility for them (a factor of particular significance following the flood disaster). Apartment transfers within the project at first were permitted for any tenant, but later limited to the physically handicapped.[8]

General rules applying to outdoor areas included: parking only in the parking lots, no parking of equipment in non-operating condition, parking of trailers and trailer houses only while loading or unloading, a twenty-mile-per-hour speed limit, and no solicitors or salesmen within the limits of Vanport City without a permit from the general manager.[9]

Originally dogs were to be kept on a leash, with state licenses (through Multnomah County) required. Apparently (as in most cities), efforts at dog control were not very successful. Complaints were frequent. The commissioners made special requests to the sheriff's office for enforcement and asked the humane society to function as they would elsewhere in Multnomah County—finally, however, they gave it up as a bad job, warning that rodent control poison used in the project frequently killed the dogs, and that if the animals caused a disturbance the owner could be evicted.[10]

Lining up to pay the weekly rent. (OHS neg. 68822)

Because Vanport City was not incorporated, the rules and regulations of HAP did not carry the weight of municipal law. Thus the only possible penalty was eviction, although HAP could attempt to collect damages or other charges. The greatest number of tenant complaints revolved around the late rent payment charge, although the unrepaired broken windows received considerable mention. One of the tenants finally got results when he wrote to his ex-senator in Texas, who referred his complaint to the national commissioner. However, most of the objectors did not have a very good case, except perhaps for occasional work schedule problems. One tenant, protesting damage charges, wrote: "As we have six small children and both [are] working, naturally this apartment could not be left in an absolutely new condition." [11]

In 1944 Victoria and Robert Ormond Case submitted an article to the *Saturday Evening Post* entitled "They Tried Utopia—And Didn't Like It." It vigorously attacked what the authors saw as regimentation and its destructive effect on the quality of life at Vanport. They held the plethora of rules responsible for the heavy exodus from the city and its "unsettling" impact on emotional security. Vanport was deemed a bureaucratic dream built with unlimited funds, and upon leaving the project, the story's central figure, called the "articulate man," stated that "it's like getting out of jail." The article was colorfully written and the *Post* accepted it, probably because of the national attention Vanport City had received. But it sent the article to the U.S. Maritime Commission for verification, and from there it found its way to HAP. [12]

The Housing Authority of Portland immediately set to work either to change the article's position or kill it. A letter attacking the story and its authors assured the Curtis Publishing Company that Vanport was not a bureaucratic dream built with unlimited funds, but simple, economical housing that solved both a traffic and critical materials problem. Inspectors only entered your home (whether you were there or not) at reasonable times, and grandma should stay home during the war anyway, instead of trying to visit you. Whatever regimentation existed was to allow the tenants to lead decent, comfortable, satisfied lives.[13]

Buried beneath all the rhetoric was a relevant issue that needed examination, although it is doubtful any conclusive determination could have been made. Fortunately for HAP, however, one of the article's basic figures was wrong: the authors had cited total move-out from all HAP projects in the Portland area for that at Vanport City. This helped HAP's defense; publication of the article was finally suspended.[14]

Attempting to discourage criticism of Vanport, HAP officials claimed that it interfered with the war effort. Even Harry Freeman succumbed in one instance. In 1943 the Catholic magazine *Extension* printed a critical commentary on living conditions in Vanport. Writing to the magazine, Freeman replied that Vanport had a staff of 840 "to look after safety, comfort, and welfare of the residents," and the tenants were as "contented . . . as war conditions permit." In addition they were of the type "who do not let personal inconvenience interfere with the larger issues," while the critics did, "with most disastrous results to the war effort."[15]

MAINTENANCE

Maintenance at Vanport City quickly became a huge operation, perhaps the biggest job of this nature in the United States. The Housing Authority provided the water supply, sewer system, electric lines to the buildings, streets, sidewalks and parking lots. About the only exceptions in utilities were the few administration telephones (during the war) and the high power lines maintained by Portland General Electric—but even here HAP owned the poles. Five wells from 115 to 152 feet deep supplied the water, held in five storage tanks 95 feet high. All sewage wastes were pumped, untreated, over the dike into the Columbia River, a fact officials liked to treat lightly. Forty-two miles of asphalt sidewalks lined the project plus eight miles of wooden walks where site conditions made heavier construction impractical.[16]

The wartime problems of securing and storing an adequate coal supply dominated the meetings of the HAP commissioners. Many difficulties in the fuel's purchase, delivery and storage were encountered. Fires broke out in the stockpile when dry coal drawing moisture from the ground generated enough heat to ignite spontaneously. Dry ice had to be used for control. The insurance company threatened cancellation, maintaining the 22,000-ton pile was too large—and 10,000 more were already on order. But, an even greater problem was the coal's low quality. No extra capacity had been built into the heating system design, and even the best fuel, with high BTU content, would barely do the job under normal weather conditions. During the latter part of the project's life, tenants who lived in units with individual space heaters were permitted to procure their own coal with a corresponding rent reduction.[17]

Some maintenance problems arose even before there was major occupancy. Furniture for the apartments arrived in such bad condition that the maintenance department predicted that when Vanport City was in full operation it would be difficult to repair the furniture as fast as it fell apart. Dinette tables were wobbly, chairs came apart, divans were weak, mirrors fell out and were of poor glass, box springs broke, and mattresses sagged.[18]

When Vanport City was turned over to HAP in mid-August, the maintenance division under O.K. Tichenor furnished some interesting and impressive statistics. Heat and hot water use was estimated at 40,000 tons of coal a year; at $14.50 a ton this would cost $558,000.

The 1943 electric power bill alone would total $144,000, while their total departmental budget was $1,478,494. Of the 630 full-time employees, 30 stayed busy keeping Vanport's garbage cans washed and disinfected.[19]

Vanport's 125 mechanics included: 26 carpenters (three of whom worked full time repairing furniture); 20 electricians who handled sewage pumps, water pumps, 1,200 electric motors and 10,500 electric stoves (10 men worked full time on the stoves—any broken stove to be replaced immediately by one that had been repaired); 15 plumbers; three water testers who checked the water every hour around the clock; 10 painters (one of their chief jobs was continually repainting the fronts of the service rooms where 35 tons of coal were unloaded into each bunker each month); a sign painter; an upholsterer; and two glaziers.[20]

One hundred seventy-eight maids cleaned and disinfected vacated apartments and the 183 laundry rooms while also doing the janitorial work in the five schoolhouses, the recreation buildings and the offices. Finally, there were 88 furnace firemen, nine steam men, and four window washers. Ten foremen supervised the maintenance employees. The complaint department remained open 24 hours a day, and the week before the above figures were issued, had received 596 complaints involving electrical work, 458 requiring carpentry, 453 plumbing problems, 138 broken windows, 65 lost keys, and 421 miscellaneous problems.[21] One of the HAP commissioners questioned the publication of these figures by the maintenance department, concerned lest they give an impression of plush service and HAP boastfulness about the large sums being spent. Another commissioner felt it produced the wrong psychological picture, that of humoring tenants.[22]

Maintenance problems continued throughout the life of the project. Whether they were excessive, considering the wartime period and built-in limitations of the project, remains inconclusive. From the first winter on, heating difficulties were a principal source of tenant complaints. On his own initiative the regional director sent two investigators and then recommended the firing of the heating engineer, which had already been done by HAP. Many complaints were in regard to the heat being turned off at night (to preserve the overloaded system), which made the apartments uncomfortable for graveyard and swing shift workers. Some tenants attempted to secure portable oil heaters and fuel oil coupons.[23]

Money sometimes was not budgeted or assigned to what HAP officials regarded as non-essentials. For example, although a real attempt had been made to landscape the project during the construction period, with over $167,000 invested in lawns, trees, and shrubs, no adequate maintenance was provided. As early as the spring of 1944 the landscape engineer complained that the skeleton grounds crew was only one-third the necessary size and not a single supervisor had any horticultural experience. So instead of the beauty spot a good crew could make it, Vanport now had the aforementioned "ratty look."[24]

Two major sewage problems occurred, aside from the accepted dumping of raw sewage into the Columbia River. The first resulted from the use during construction of a light one-eighth-inch thick, second-hand sewer pipe salvaged from a defunct hydraulic mining operation in California. Run through a culvert under the tracks of the North Portland Terminal Company, it broke inside the culvert several times. When this happened the pumps had to be shut down, sewage overflowed into the sloughs on the projects, and because of the slow drainage the water remained polluted for weeks. Permanent repairs were finally made in 1944. Vanport sewage entering Oregon Slough above the large Swift packing plant's water supply intake created the second problem. Sewage entered its boilers and wash water supply, causing a quiet controversy that was still continuing in 1945. Whether any solution was reached before the flood remains unknown.[25] Fortunately for HAP neither got much public attention.

The Housing Authority of Portland and the FPHA became concerned with the excessive cost and possible inefficiency of the maintenance operation. In early February 1944 they tried to reduce its cost by one-third while upgrading service. The staff was reduced from approximately 850 to slightly less than 700, and further reductions were hoped for. Later some of the commissioners, anonymously touring the project, reported a great deal of loafing and commented that they would hate to be a tenant at Vanport trying to deal with the maintenance service. Vanport officials maintained the commissioners did not really understand the problem.[26]

COMMERCIAL SERVICES

Commercial services were operated in Housing Authority buildings under a percentage contract with HAP. This involved an astonishing amount of time and detail which ordinarily would have been handled privately. In the beginning every sort of business operation required a lease and in many instances a sublease. A resolution of the board of commissioners eventually permitted smaller operations and finally some of these were put on month by month contracts by spoken agreement. However, all required HAP approval, including popcorn wagons, shoeshine stands, and the sale of Christmas trees and "Pronto Pups." Files had to be maintained on all operations. Besides covering the ordinary wide range of business services, these same contractual procedures applied to individual medical and dental services carried on outside the hospital. Because of the wartime shortage HAP even sold lightbulbs until they again became generally available.[27]

With Vanport's population already in the 10,000 range, the first and largest of five commercial centers

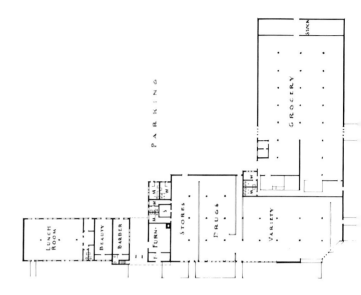

Wolff and Phillips rendering of Shopping Center No. 1 (OHS neg. 68794)

opened 8 April 1943. Oregon Groceteria Company ran the food market. There was a combination drug, general merchandise, and clothing store. The restaurant seated almost 400 diners and operated 24-hours a day. An 80-stool lunch counter, also carrying tobacco and magazines, and a barber shop, beauty parlor and laundry depot completed the installation. Commerical Center Number 2 started operation the following August, but more were desperately needed, for which HAP endeavored to obtain authorization. In 1944 three small ones were built, completing the number the project would have. There never was a bank, but checks could be cashed at one of the commercial buildings.[28]

The Housing Authority of Portland provided almost all of the institutions of community life in Vanport City, either directly or through contractual lease. Exceptions were postal service, bus service, and Multnomah County health and welfare services.

38

Police protection was furnished through contract with the Multnomah County Sheriff's Office. Ard M. Pratt, appointed chief deputy in charge of Vanport, became, in effect, its police chief. During 1947, in an effort to increase security, seven HAP watchmen were deputized and worked at Vanport under the sheriff's office. The police office also served as a telegraph station after normal hours. A special police building constructed in 1944 included a jail that served mainly as a drunk tank and for temporary holding until prisoners could be transferred to other county facilities. At first, traffic law enforcement proved difficult; whether the Stop and No Parking signs were legal was uncertain as the streets had not been deeded to the county. Authorities finally discovered that an Oregon law could be used to cover the situation and enforcement thereafter proceeded on a more secure basis.[29]

At first, some friction did develop between HAP and the sheriff's office. In general the commissioners wished to have more say in the conduct of law enforcement policies, while the Multnomah County police administration, feeling they understood the job much better,

A branch fire station in Vanport. (OHS neg. 68820)

was not about to take orders from HAP. At one point the commissioners debated using the funds paid the county to establish their own system, but friction subsequently lessened and relations remained quite amicable through the duration of the project's life.[30]

The Housing Authority of Portland maintained and operated its own fire department. It consisted of three stations, seven trucks, and about 60 full-time firemen. Emergency alarm boxes hung on the power poles. The Portland Fire Department agreed to provide assistance in the event HAP felt a fire was beyond its control. The later *Resident Handbook* blandly stated, "Your Vanport Fire Department is the best in the country."[31] Because of the compactness of the project the department at least was close to any fire that might break out.

In October 1942 HAP did contact the United States Post Office for aid in designing the building to be used for its activities. However, Vanport had approximately 10,000 residents before regular United States Postal Service became available. Originally Project Manager J. L. Franzen picked up the mail at the Kenton Post Office, and 10 HAP employees delivered it. Finally, on 29 March 1943, the new post office opened. Mail was delivered directly from the main Portland station and excepting general delivery all regular services were instituted.[32] Apparently the postal department did not relish the potential massive headaches created by general delivery service to such a fluid population.

It took even longer for bus service to commence. Portland Traction Company eventually asked the Portland City Council for approval of a bus route to Vanport City, which it granted on 8 April 1943. By May buses were running every 30 minutes, and eventually every ten. The Multnomah County Health Department started its operation in Vanport as early as January 1943, holding a smallpox and diphtheria clinic, an aspect of disease control felt to be especially vital because of the anticipated density of population.[33]

HOSPITAL SERVICES

Vanport Hospital was a first class facility, designed by the project's general architects and modeled on a smaller scale after the Permanente Foundation Hospital in Vancouver. Begun in late February 1943, construction was complete before July of that year and the entire hospital, including the out-patient section, was operating by 2 August. Although deemed a temporary structure, it became a fine 150-bed establishment with medical, maternity, isolation, and nursery sections, and had a full complement of operating rooms and clinics. It was capable of being used by a capacity staff of 100, including doctors, nurses, and attendants. The Multnomah County Health Department was also located in the building. The walk-in prescription business became the one area of operations that never grew to be a problem, since the hospital prided itself on selling below the prices that were charged in Portland and even in other dispensaries in Vanport.[34]

From start to finish the Vanport Hospital proved to be a thorn in the administration's side. The principal difficulty was that both doctors and paying patients were hard to find. The Housing Authority of Portland envisaged an operation by the Oregon Physicians' Service (OPS) similar to that being conducted in their other hospitals, and a contract was signed with them in late March. Oregon Physician's Service anticipated such a great demand that it insisted on a rider releasing the service from liability if all facilities in Portland and Vanport were fully occupied. It would compensate the subscriber with money equivalent to the lost services up to $100 ($5.00 per day was the going room rate). Oregon Physician's Service made attempts to sign up Vanporters for the OPS plan, but it soon became apparent that tenants were not buying in sufficient numbers so OPS was authorized to operate the hospital on the open (fee-for-service) plan.[35]

Troubles arose almost immediately. Two months

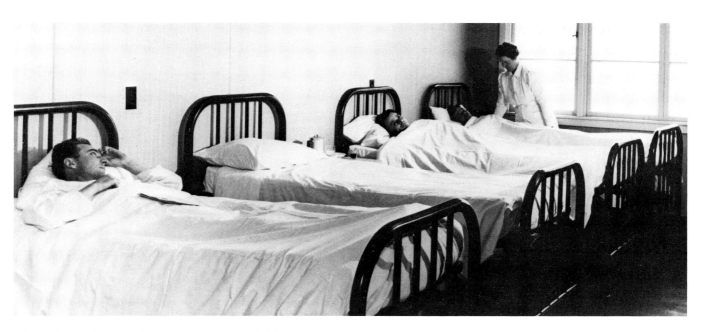

Kaiser hospital room at Vanport. (OHS neg. 71104)

after the hospital opened, OPS reported a $26,000 deficit. At the time it claimed the loss was due to a lack of some types of equipment, which it wanted the housing authority to provide, but no assurance was given. Complicating the issue, Lanham Act funds would finance only a non-profit operation. By December 1943, OPS demanded that the losses be underwritten. In addition the need for a standby power plant became obvious as emergency operations had been performed by flashlight. The losses continued in January, and OPS began to organize a non-profit operation in order to qualify for federal funds. In mid-May OPS notified HAP of termination of the old contract, and on 1 June 1944, OPS requested deficit funds from HAP while waiting on its federal application. This request was granted, and HAP executed a lease with the new non-profit corporation.[36]

In the midst of these difficulties Harry Freeman wrote a confidential letter to the Seattle office stating his fear that OPS might abandon Vanport, giving as its reason HAP's refusal to sponsor the OPS membership plan. Going unmentioned by OPS, according to Freeman, were these factors: Portland hospitals would not accept Vanport Hospital because of the "taint of socialized medicine" which made it almost impossible to attract staff doctors to Vanport; furthermore doctors in Vanport City sent patients to overcrowded Portland hospitals while the one in Vanport stood vacant. The Housing Authority of Portland must consider alternatives, he wrote, such as U.S. Public Health Service operation, a doctor draft, or something similar to Kaiser's Permanente Foundation.[37]

Because of the early financial difficulties OPS became overly concerned about patient payment. If an injury was not too serious, as in the case of one man with

41

Management Division Director, Kenneth E. Eckert. (*From Roses to Rivets*)

burns on the face and neck, the hospital's stance was cash now or no help. Another factor that caused OPS some unhappiness, was that until the jail facilities were completed the hospital had to take the drunks picked up by the police.[38]

Lanham Act funds were obtained, but the dearth of physicians and surgeons worsened during the winter of 1944–45. Only part-time doctors were available, and there was constant turnover. A letter from the hospital superintendent to HAP Management Division Director Kenneth E. Eckert starkly outlined the dilemma: an army physician from a Vancouver installation, moonlighting for six hours a night and on Sunday was the only thing keeping the hospital going (this, he explained, was against army regulations so it should not be mentioned); on Sundays there were 40,000 people absolutely devoid of doctors except for him. If the nine doctors in Vanport worked full time (and they did not) the doctor-patient ratio would be 1 to 4,500, probably the worst in the United States. A man had just died without being able to secure any medical attention (two interns busy in surgery were the only staff there). An epidemic would result in a national scandal. The Medical Society of Multnomah County would not help. The only hope was action on the national level.[39]

Some amelioration of the physicians crisis occurred after the war, but in the spring of 1946 FPHA's regional office announced suspension of federal funds for the hospital and schools. The *Oregonian* angrily accused them of trying to disown Vanport City. Immediately another crisis began building, and reached a head in late 1946. On 24 October a special meeting of HAP Commissioners, the medical staff, and others aired the problem. There were larger collection losses than from other hospitals. Patients other hospitals suspected of not being able to pay were sent to Vanport on the excuse their facility was full. On 7 November, the commissioners suggested newspaper publicity of the excellent facilities.[40]

In another meeting, held 15 November, those assembled felt that a 100 patient average would make the hospital self-supporting if the present deluxe operation was tightened up. At present it had too many nurses, nurses aides, and office personnel. Cuts were decided on and hope of Community Chest support entertained. Still another meeting was held with the Multnomah County Medical Society who believed that although reductions would help, as long as it was considered temporary, the hospital could never be made self-supporting. The crisis continued. Because of the terminations the remaining employees were looking for new jobs; the heating system was not economical; and without philanthropic assistance the hospital would have to close at the end of the year. Someone suggested an appeal to the President of the United States, basing it on Vanport's large veteran population.[41]

The commissioners were desperate. Freeman offered the building to the practicing doctors in Vanport City for $1 a year if they would take over. There was no response. The many attempts, petitions, appeals had all failed, and the government continued to stand firm. Only the offer by the Kaiser Company's hospital in Vancouver (Northern Permanente Foundation), to take over operation for $1 a year plus the cost of utilities saved the institution's closure, but this did not completely end HAP's involvement. The old non-profit Vanport Hospital Association wanted some of the equipment back. Harry Freeman felt that since it had been purchased out of income and the Federal Works Administration (FWA) had made up the deficit, the Association did not have a right to it. Old medical records (OPS did not take them) had to be stored and when needed for court cases, resulted in frequent subpoenas.[42]

Permanente soon found it could not break even. Hospital occupancy was at 50 percent, with a loss of $5,000 a month. Throughout its term of operation Permanente did a lot of charity work, and never refused a patient. After being subsidized for over a year, Permanente requested permission to operate the hospital as an out-patient clinic and emergency department only, longer term patients to be transferred to the Vancouver facility. On 6 May 1948, the change was approved, and the transfers then effected—fortunate timing, as the flood came on 30 May.[44]

The whole story of the hospital had a loser-like quality typical of Vanport. A planner's idea, designed to improve the quality of life for war workers and their families, it contained all the ingredients of success except participation of the people involved, residents and doctors alike. It failed, but in failing laid another building block in a structure that has yet to be finished—adequate medical care for all the people of the United States.

LIBRARY SERVICES

As with so many aspects of Vanport, the public library was unique. Designed in Vanport's original plans, it was the only public library in the United States within a war housing project. It stood on Victory Boulevard next to the fire station, its glass and brick supporting wall exterior providing a pleasant contrast to the wooden apartments. Opened in July 1943, the facility operated under the school district with Portland Library Association supervision; the Lanham Act provided the operating funds. Furnished with borrowed school furniture, 1,000 books from the Portland Library supplemented its own stock. Only adults and high school students were allowed to use the facility.[45]

Originally the librarians planned to issue Portland Public Library cards, but quickly dropped this idea because most Vanporters could not give local references, so the library issued its own cards, without references. Reading tastes in Vanport did not differ significantly from those in most other places; best sellers, mysteries, and westerns were popular. The combination of demand and short supply necessitated a limit of three books per person. Sheriff's office deputies helped circulation by picking up books more than 10 days overdue during their regular rounds.[46]

Lanham Act funds were withdrawn in September 1944. The Housing Authority tried to convince Multnomah County to finance the library operation. The county replied that funds for this purpose were not in the budget, and the 10 mill county levy (not collected in Vanport) could hardly be used. The Authority's at-

Attorney for HAP, Lester W. Humphreys (OHS neg. 69457)

torney, Lester W. Humphreys, suggested HAP operate the library and deduct the cost from the in-lieu-of-tax payment made to the county. Operation was finally stabilized with FPHA authorizing HAP to carry the librarians on its payroll, while the Library Association of Portland served as administrator, operating the library as its largest branch.[47]

The Housing Authority of Portland maintained a Project Services Department at Vanport City. Although it had certain vague areas of responsibility (morale, public health, and welfare), it mainly dealt with recreation, church, and club activities.[48] Between this department and the public schools, children and teenagers were provided with an exceptionally fine recreational program. Unfortunately, programs for Vanport's adult population were less satisfactory, although adequate space was furnished for church and club meetings.

The first and largest of the five recreation buildings, Recreation Center Number 1, opened quietly on 4 May 1943, the Portland Park Bureau's traveling caravan of entertainers providing entertainment. The official opening took place 18 May, with around 3,000 people in attendance. Johnny Carpenter of KOIN radio (who had a long career in Portland's public eye) prepared the script. A concert and a dance followed the radio program. Almost 90 yards long and over 100 feet wide, and containing social rooms, club rooms, a game room, lounge, assembly room, and a gymnasium, the building seemed enormous. Two nursery school buildings later were converted to recreation centers. All were adequately staffed with competent personnel. There were also 15 playgrounds, two "major" size ball parks, several small softball diamonds, and 10 acres of parks with benches, lawns, and a foot bridge and diving float at Force Lake Park.[49]

At first the Portland Park Bureau operated the recreational program, but HAP established a new organizational structure in January 1945. A committee of Vanport citizens formed the Vanport Recreation Association and received a Lanham Act grant to conduct the program until the end of the fiscal year. A letter to the Association from HAP Management Director, Kenneth E. Eckert (Freeman's chief assistant), dated 29 May indi-

Vanport Library (OHS neg. CN 006811)

cated HAP's dissatisfaction with the Association's operation. Eckert acknowledged the difficulties of wartime staffing but stated that due to the "type of physical living" at Vanport, a better staff and program was especially necessary.[50]

The Vanport Recreation Association did not take this criticism lightly, strongly disagreeing with HAP over its effectiveness in operating eight community buildings and 15 play areas. By September it notified HAP it was disbanding and wished to dispose of the equipment to the Authority or the public schools. The Housing Authority requested that the board of directors resign after electing a new board, in order to leave the organizational structure intact. They refused and HAP desperately tried to get another formed, believing that abandonment would lead to unrest or, even worse, racial problems. It appealed to FWA to transfer funds and equipment, and to FPHA about the great need for the program—in its absence juvenile delinquency would rise, fires would be started; increased thievery had already begun. It all came to naught, and funding to pay personnel was disapproved.

Another appeal in December met the same fate despite HAP's assurance that another group wished to continue the program. The Portland Council of Social Agencies sent a special entreaty. But the federal goose that laid the wartime golden eggs stopped laying, and adjustment to this new condition was difficult.[51]

The chief recreational problem at Vanport was the almost total lack of commercial, adult amusement facilities. The single theater seated approximately 750 people. Its double-feature program which changed three times a week had to accommodate 40,000 people in an era when movie going was extremely popular. There was not a single poolhall, card room, bowling alley or beer parlor. The Housing Authority Board of Commissioners, with their "big brother" solicitude for the morals of Vanport residents, several times refused requests to sell draft beer. A few pinball games were operated in Commerical Center Number 1. Consequently,

Exterior view of Recreation Building #1. The use of brick facing was unusual in Vanport. (OHS neg. 68801)

almost from the very beginning, apartments were secretly used for "blind pig joints" (speakeasies), crap games, and other forms of gambling.[52]

The Housing Authority consistently turned down other proposals for commercial recreation. As early as 1943 an application to outfit a penny arcade was refused. Because they thought that it would be noisy and a nuisance, the commissioners discouraged establishment of a small amusement park, which would have contained a merry-go-round and carnival booths, on private land on the project's north side. Later on they bewailed the lack of adult recreation and proposed moving a large building from a Vancouver housing project to be converted for commercial, adult recreation uses but federal approval could never be secured. After 1945 HAP allowed the Multnomah County Sheriff's Band to sponsor a yearly carnival (West Coast Shows).[53]

There were no churches in Vanport. Religious activities were provided for by working through the Portland United Church Ministry, the Catholic Committee, and the Jewish Council, who together provided a staff of resident ministers. Services were scheduled in one of the community buildings and all of the schools. Until the school conflicts of Vanport's last years, church activities accounted for most of the project's limited community participation.[54]

A NEWSPAPER FOR VANPORT

Attempts to establish a successful newspaper proved abortive until late 1947, and then HAP did not like the paper's independent stance. As early as June 1943, City Manager J.L. Franzen and Executive Director Harry Freeman were talking of a newspaper. The publisher of the Gresham, Oregon *Outlook* had proposed to the board of commissioners a weekly paper for Vanport, with an accompanying subsidy from HAP until the paper became self-supporting. K.E. Eckert pointed out that every housing project in the United States except Vanport City had a newspaper. The proposal split the commissioners, and raised the question of adequate *Oregonian* and *Journal* coverage. A committee was appointed to meet with Harry Freeman and study the proposition; it concluded that a newspaper was desirable but probably could not be subsidized. The Federal Public Housing Administration suggested working out a contract and submitting it to the Seattle office, but did not hold out much hope as Washington was now making an effort to suspend publications.[55]

The commissioners debated the issue into July. Unwilling to expend $1,000 per week while the project continued as a deficit operation, Chairman C.M. Gartrell suggested that a smaller community news and activities publication would suffice. Commissioner C.A. Moores argued that a newspaper would create a community atmosphere and develop civic pride. By a vote of three to two, it was decided to submit the proposal to the regional director for approval. It eventually reached Washington, D.C. and was rejected in August. This first attempt died with the commissioners speculating on the possibility of Edgar Kaiser as a financing angel.[56]

A year later, August 1944, a local printing agency proposed a shopping newspaper with a front page prepared by HAP. The application was not considered after an unfavorable credit report on the agency. By 1946 the only publication was an amateur, mimeographed news sheet done on eight-and-one-half by eleven inch paper by teen-age volunteers working in an activity program under the Project Services' staff. It struggled along, got publicity in the Oregon *Journal*, changed its name to *Voice of Vanport*, became four pages, was multilithed instead of mimeographed, and then succumbed in the late summer of 1947.[57]

The only publication in Vanport that ever remotely resembled a newspaper appeared in the fall of 1947 as a joint venture of HAP and Ralph Bennett. Bennett had worked on the Harvard *Crimson*, then had returned

The Lounge Room in Recreation Building #1. (OHS neg. 68802)

to The Dalles, Oregon to operate his father's weekly paper. After the paper was sold he worked for the Bonneville Power Administration Information Division but his job was terminated because of budget reductions. From there he came to the HAP as a Project Services' employee.[58]

In a memorandum to Vanport City Manager Harry D. Jaeger, Bennett sketched out his plans. A commitment for up to 16 pages had been secured from the printer. The first weekly issue was to be published 12 September 1947. Six full size pages were hoped for (it turned out to be four). It was to be addressed by volunteers (using HAP equipment), mailed, with Friday morning delivery promised. The *Voice of Vanport* bank balance would be utilized, along with the editor's own funds. The paper would be adult and eventually self-supporting. It was not to be an amateur effort with a "juvenile point of view;" the traditions of the "best journalism" would prevail, and its editorials would focus on creating a feeling of citizenship in Vanport. Local issues were to be examined—the schools, the United States Senate housing investigation, and the future of Vanport. When and if the paper became profitable, Bennett would take over publication, continuing to allow HAP censorship of news and editorial policy. How this last squared with the traditions of the "best journalism" was not mentioned. Finally, Bennett maintained, the operation under the present arrangement would be less expensive to HAP than the *Voice of Vanport* had been.[59]

The new Vanport *Tribune* quickly met with mixed reaction. Commissioner H.J. Detloff wondered when it was going to have more news, claiming it was too much like a "throw away." Soon he became openly critical of the paper's unfavorable publicity on HAP policies. Harry Freeman reported the first four issues had made money, money which would help to defray the expenses of HAP employees working on it, and the paper might soon be able to go to six pages. The commissioners decided to keep the paper operating but admonished Bennett to check any policy matters with Freeman.[60]

Vanport merchants liked the new paper. They felt there was a great response to their advertising. When a Mr. Green proposed to HAP that it replace the Vanport *Tribune* with a tabloid published by him at no cost to the Authority, the merchants objected and agreed to pay for more advertising so Bennett could run the paper on his own, although they did oppose advertising from outside Vanport. Harry Jaeger reported the *Tribune* publicized project information more effectively than had ever been done before. But in spite of these recommendations and HAP attorney Lester W. Humphreys' reminder that although the opportunity for a newspaper in Vanport had been open since 1942 no interest had been shown by responsible parties, the board of commissioners voted unanimously to cancel the paper on 1 January 1948, and invited new proposals for running one. Commissioner Detloff again remarked on the poor job of censorship. Whether a protest by the Allied Printing Trades Council over use of HAP addressograph equipment and mailing by non-union members entered into the decision remains unclear.[61]

The only person to submit a proposal was Ralph Bennett. Grudgingly the commissioners gave in; one commissioner got in a last criticism of a bingo advertisement. There was to be no direct aid from HAP or financial responsibility to it. An elaborate lease was drawn, to be approved by the San Francisco office; HAP supplied a room in Recreation Center Number 1 for a $1 yearly rent, while declaring its approval contingent upon the lessee refraining from commenting on political or "other controversial questions." Five months later the flood would eliminate both Vanport and the paper.[62]

ADMINISTRATIVE DETAILS

In addition to the major problems facing HAP there were a host of miscellaneous problems involved in administrative details. For instance, in the very beginning, single men who arrived without funds were lodged at Vanport and put to work at Oregon Shipbuilding Corporation. This necessitated an elaborate bookkeeping system for advance payroll deductions good for rent and for meal tickets at the Vanport Cafeteria. Also, HAP had trouble getting out the huge maintenance payroll under the early, more chaotic administrative conditions. Shifting government attitudes caused frustration. Originally the cafeterias were directed to provide wholesome food with no concern for profit. In early 1945 this policy changed to insistence on an overall profitable project operation, but cafeteria workers' wages were to be increased and food prices were to remain constant. To resolve this dilemma HAP refused to consider pinballs and beer as an additional income source, suggesting instead to FPHA the raising of project rents, an action that presumably, would be less harmful to morale. Excessive cashier's shortages occurred constantly at Vanport, another indication that Vanport was unusual in even the most minor things.[63]

Another detail was the constant tenant demand for larger quarters or for permission to move to another area of the project. In the postwar period some of the veterans attending Vanport College became irritated when their requests for larger quarters were refused, believing that apartments to fit their needs were available. Charges were made—some a little wild. One veteran claimed there were 5,000 vacancies. Another who lived with his parents in a two room apartment kept badgering the administration for a three room apartment in order to study more effectively. Finally he was told nothing short of an order from the president of the United States would secure him one. So he wrote to President Truman. Whether he obtained the larger quarters is not known, but the letter finally found its way back to HAP, and the Authority had to justify its position.

However, there do not appear to have been a large

Q. B. Griffin. (OHS neg. 69469)

number of complaints about the administration of Vanport. Whether this was due solely to general satisfaction or in part because of the less-than-average literacy of the project's inhabitants would be impossible to say.[64]

During Vanport's first year of operation some friction arose between the management at the city and segments of the top administration. This situation is revealed in the 1943 HAP minutes where there are references to tenant complaints, "skips" and increased turnover, and to the Seattle office's intervention in connection with heating problems. In February 1944, one of the commissioners mounted an attack on Manager J.L. Franzen, whom, he declared, had declined help in meeting administrative problems ("help" meaning the attempt to force Q.B. Griffin on him as his assistant). The Housing Authority's executive director replied that it was true that Franzen had not been attending to directives. The management director, however, reported that Franzen had now changed his attitude, agreed he needed assistance, and would accept Griffin. This apparently satisfied the critical commissioner. However, Franzen was vigorously supported by another commissioner. Franzen's side of the dispute remains untold but perhaps included his analysis of the commissioners' insistence on citizen participation, an effort Franzen felt would fail—his evaluation turned out to be correct. At any rate, in September 1944, about six months after the dispute came to a head Franzen resigned, declaring that since the Vanport administration was now well established he could return to the pressing needs of Oregon City. Housing Authority officials contributed the usual syrupy statement about Franzen's services. Q.B. Griffin stepped up into the manager's role, remaining there until 30 April 1946, when he was succeeded by Harry D. Jaeger.[65]

POSTWAR VANPORT

In spite of all the wartime administrative difficulties, the commissioners did concern themselves with the problem of what would happen to Vanport when the war ended. There was never any consideration of permanency. The Lanham Act under which the project funds finally were obtained called for demolition or removal, while the National Housing Act stated federally owned houses were to be disposed of in the public interest. As early as May 1943 Portland City Commissioner William Bowes advised HAP officials that Portland was opposed to FPHA sale of parts or whole projects for living units. Executive Secretary Harry Freeman replied that National Housing Association officials were preparing an amendment to the act making disposition even more iron-clad. Chairman C.M. Gartrell had expressed the general opinion when at the 12 August opening ceremonies he had accepted the Vanport lease with the statement, "Temporary though the facilities may be. . . ."[66]

The first talk of moving some units to California occurred as early as June 1944. This proposal had hardly faded away when in October, HAP received an unexpected directive from FPHA to terminate 56 units at Vanport. The directive elicited a rather huffy response, and HAP sent a telegram to FPHA headquarters requesting a policy delineation between locals and FPHA as far as reprogramming was concerned.[67] It soon became clear that Edgar Kaiser had proposed the demolition of Vanport, and the metamorphosis of the area into a permanent residential-industrial development. He had discussed this plan with the mayor of Portland and then sent a representative to Washington, D.C. to talk with the head of FPHA, who told the representative to go back and work out a plan with the community. Kaiser representatives subsequently proposed to the commissioners that an XYZ corporation be formed to oversee the development of several hundred permanent homes and 380 acres for industrial purposes. The houses were to be built by private enterprise through contract with the National Housing Administration (NHA). Kaiser Company was not to be involved in the building, and any profit accruing to the XYZ corporation would go to charity. According to the company if some such plan were not adopted Vanport would turn into a slum.[68]

During most of the previous part of 1944, HAP com-

Herbert J. Dahlke. He led the drive for post-war use of Vanport as a servicemen's rehabilitation center. He succeeded Chester A. Moores as chairman of the Board of Commissioners. (*From Roses to Rivets*)

were the local Apartment House Owner's Association and home building interests. On the horns of a dilemma, they approved the planned industry features but did not want the home building, and yet felt somewhat reluctant to drive Kaiser out of the community. As usual, immediate self-interest prevailed.[69]

The Housing Authority of Portland made its deci-

Chester A. Moores succeeded C. M. Gartrell as Chairman of the Board of Commissioners of HAP. Moores led the drive to turn Vanport into an industrial site after the war. (OHS neg. 54302)

missioners, led by Herbert Dahlke, had been promoting the postwar use of the Vanport site for a servicemen's rehabilitation center. Correspondence regarding this had been sent to various public officials. The Kaiser Company now informed HAP that the Army, Navy, and Veteran's Administration did not approve of the location, and if the Kaiser plan was not approved they would have to withdraw from future operational planning for the Portland area. Lined up in opposition to the Kaiser plan sion. It dropped the rehabilitation plan, having received no encouragement, and shifted to promoting the Vanport site for strictly industrial use. Housing units at Vanport should be demolished as they became vacant, and HAP should handle the disposal. The decision effectively stopped the Kaiser plan, which was shelved in Washington, D.C. for future study. However, HAP's lease from FPHA was amended to make it clear that neither had ultimate jurisdiction in disposal or demolition; that decision would rest with NHA.[70] Whether the Kaiser Company eventually would have made Portland a major base, had a different approach been taken, must remain forever in the realm of speculation. Except for Northern Permanente Foundation, a hospital-medical insurance plan, it wound up any large scale operation with the war's end, not exercising an option it apparently had to acquire the Vanport community.[71]

From late 1944 until the spring of 1946 a great deal of activity was aimed at winding up the project and putting the area to some future use, activity that did not end until the postwar housing shortage developed. Commissioner Chester A. Moores, who succeeded C.M. Gartrell as HAP chairman upon the latter's resignation, led the drive to convert Vanport into an industrial area. The Housing Authority asked FPHA to approve its request to the Port of Portland to study the possibility of dredging a deepwater channel into the area. Wayne Morse, Oregon's new senator-elect, was planning a trip to Washington at his own expense to promote industrialization of Vanport as the key to Portland's industrial future. Studies for foundation investigation and industrial possibilities were commissioned.[72]

Heavy occupancy reoccurred in 1945 and somewhat dampened prospects but Moores continued his hard campaign. In June he traveled to Washington, D.C. to argue for the plan, claiming that a large plant had recently located in Seattle because available sites in the Portland area lacked visibility from a major arterial highway, a quality Vanport had in abundance. The original low purchase price of $350 an acre made it possible to sell the land cheaply. He argued, with little success, for greater local control of disposition when the need for a project ended.[73]

The bureaucratic procedures for disposal were indeed cumbersome. In addition to hazy areas of responsibility, such as relocation of tenants, there was a long series of steps on any one of which a plan could easily founder. The National Housing Authority would decide on dwelling removal within two years of the wars' end unless an emergency still existed and FPHA would carry out the demolition or removal. At this time the vacated property would be declared surplus and transferred to the Surplus Property Board, which would determine to whom the land would be assigned. If the board decided the land was industrial it would go to the Reconstruction Finance Corporation (RFC) and if residential, back to FPHA. This whole process might be applied to only part of a project. Some disagreement even arose as to whether, under Oregon law, HAP could deal with land for any purpose other than housing.[74]

Moores continued the fight. He kept badgering FPHA's new regional director Jesse Epstein to try and secure RFC and NHA appraisals. He supplied already completed planning to congressional committees as grounds for disposal of the project, but in December 1945 Moores resigned, an action that must have been due in part to his frustration. By the spring of 1946, HAP quit the struggle, and aside from leasing a small amount of building space for minor operations (manufacture of artificial limbs and water softening machines), the battle to convert Vanport to industrial use was over.[75]

As shipyard operations began to wind down in 1945 some unit removal occurred. In June NHA suggested to HAP that 1,200 apartment units be moved to the naval yard at Bremerton, Washington to save materials; the units were not needed at Vanport as there were 4,500 vacancies in the Portland-Vancouver area. The Housing Authority did not wish to comply, perhaps foreseeing a future housing problem, and in addition, many of the reputed vacancies were not in its jurisdiction. A gradual deterioration in relations between HAP and FPHA commenced, compounded out of administrative changes at FPHA, lack of consideration of the industrial plan, and local control of issues such as disposition and racial considerations in housing assignments. After some reasonably polite arm-twisting (such as notification that it could be overruled) HAP concurred in the removal, but not without recommending a delay of six months.[76]

The Federal Public Housing Administration disregarded the recommendation for delay, and the removal process got under way, conducted from Seattle. In late July NHA requested the transfer of 500 more units, quoting the Kaiser Company and the War Manpower Commission that shipyard employment would be decreasing and the units therefore would not be needed. The Housing Authority of Portland commissioners, their vote divided, would not approve; again they were informed they could be overruled. Finally they approved 252 units. In the midst of the demolition and transfer the war ended. The last units were cancelled, but the contractor proceeded on the original 1,204, only now it was merely for salvage. So work slowed to a pace at the contractor's convenience, and Executive Director Harry Freeman was soon protesting to FPHA about the serious fire hazards and juvenile temptations from the wreckage piles, plus the ghost town appearance of buildings with doors, windows and roofs missing. The Housing Authority of Portland also requested that in case of any further termination, the local Authority be used for the actual bidding process.[77]

There was reason for HAP to oppose quick removal of parts of the project. The anticipated exodus of war workers did not occur, housing demands of military personnel increased, and discharged veterans were having trouble finding housing as were returning Portlanders who had engaged in war work elsewhere. In December 1945, a freeze order from FPHA stopped any further demolition pending an investigation to determine how many units should be transferred elsewhere for housing purposes. In 1946 the *Oregonian* joined the fight against hasty dismantling. Some removal resumed in 1946, but by March 1947 the number of dwelling units at Vanport City stabilized at 6,396 out of the original 9,942.[78]

FEDERAL VS. LOCAL

The Housing Authority of Portland faced other difficult administrative problems as a result of the end of the war, most of which arose from inconsistencies in the federal policy to which the Authority was expected to adapt. Project operation in the "black" was demanded, along with adherence to newly developing welfare conceptions as applied to public housing. A 23 August 1945 telegram from the Seattle office instructed HAP to curtail all unnecessary expenditures. This dovetailed with the commissioners' attitudes, as they had always watched carefully over the public's money and had consistently criticized the excess of personnel. They happily concurred with FPHA approval of allowing tenants to furnish their own coal, accompanied by a corresponding rental deduction, and of changing rents from a weekly to monthly basis.[79]

A confused policy developed over project residents' eligibility for public housing. The eligible industry list dropped from several hundred to only twelve, in addition to veterans, although Vanport tenants who now were no longer eligible were not to be evicted. Immediately the NHA began to feel pressure from the housing shortage. Termination of housing units stopped and around the first of November the association sent a new, rather ambiguous statement to the local authorities, granting them permission to open projects to "displaced" and "dislocated" residents. The vagueness was probably deliberate, passing the pressure and responsibility. The Housing Authority did not object.[80]

However, HAP could not reconcile a new FPHA policy of adjusted rents with the demand for a sound fiscal operation. Washington, D.C. announced a new rate schedule for both veterans and hardship (welfare) cases, which could be adopted by local authorities if they so desired. In these cases rents were to be $27 a month for a furnished unit with utilities. The Housing Authority adopted the policy for veterans only. The Vanport Tenants' League, an organization representing primarily Vanport's black population was formed to fight for adjusted rents for those who would classify as welfare cases.[81]

At a meeting of the League, President Jess Skolnick charged that HAP had not complied with an FPHA order. Herbert J. Dahlke, now chairman of the board of commissioners, and Freeman replied that the policy was not mandatory and held to their position. The League continued its attack. On 18 February 1946, an article in the *Daily People's World* charged the commissioners with representing only business interests and wanting Vanport dismantled in order to force one-third of the metropolitan area's Negroes to leave and also to force veterans to buy homes at the current high prices. Although these charges were patently untrue, HAP finally bowed to the pressure and adopted the full program in April.[82]

In September FPHA adopted a new adjusted rents policy based on income instead of the policy being applied to welfare cases and veterans. It was the forerunner of the policy in widespread use today in government housing projects and housing authority rental of private homes. Local housing authorities were directed to establish it in all projects. The Housing Authority did not wish to, feeling that if their operations had to be economically sound the adjustments for veterans and welfare cases were enough and it simply ignored the directive. Although HAP was soon charged with racial prejudice as the reason for its lack of action, evidence to support the contention was lacking.[83]

In the meantime, in a somewhat contradictory move, FPHA had notified HAP to put into effect a $2.00 increase in adjusted rents because of increased operating costs, and a legal restriction that no rent be adjusted below the average regional cost of operation. Upon sending a letter of protest to the commissioners, the League was invited to send *one* (emphasis by the author) representative to the next HAP meeting. The increased rent was protested at that time.[84]

The League finally obtained details on the new FPHA policy concerning eligibility for adjusted rent. It sent a letter and appeared at the 3 April HAP meeting, arguing for adjusted rents for non-veteran, non-welfare cases, claiming the existence of many eligible cases and pointing to the McLoughlin Heights project in adjacent Vancouver, Washington where the policy was in effect. The Housing Authority said the League would be notified of its decision, and two weeks later informed the League that any tenants who believed they were eligible could apply, and if they indeed qualified, an adjusted rent would go into effect in May. This might be mildly described as a little "foot dragging." In August, however, HAP gave up and openly adopted the schedule.[85]

The fears HAP had about large budgetary deficits were well founded. In the six month period ending 31 December 1947, its budget was out of balance by a sizable amount ($200,000) for the first time. Vanport City was the chief cause of the deficit. The in-lieu-of-tax payments to the public schools did not completely cover their operating costs but the 2,600 families (41 percent of the dwelling units) on adjusted rents were by far the main cause. It should not be assumed that the commissioners objected per se to adjusted rents, but they wished to run a financially sound operation, and many of FPHA's instructions had been to this effect. If Vanport was to be considered the "white elephant" type of project, they wanted it acknowledged.[86]

THE ACCOMPLISHMENTS OF HAP

How well did the HAP conduct this multifaceted operation, administer the best known and largest part of its empire—Vanport City? Any overall judgment that considers the time and setting must conclude that a superb job was done in running what national NHA Commissioner Philip Klutznick termed the most difficult housing project in the nation.[87] Millions of dollars were expended without the slightest hint of graft or corruption. The commissioners comprised a talent pool which would have been impossible to hire. They willingly contributed vast amounts of time with no pay, and at times absorbed much undeserved abuse. They obtained full measure for the taxpayer's dollar, and even effected some innovations within rather restrictive governmental confines. They felt a genuine concern for the residents of Vanport. During its whole history Vanport City was considered a temporary, emergency project by all, as were most of HAP's other projects; and that the commissioners shared this widespread attitude rather than developing a philosophy of permanent public housing can hardly be held against them.

Ultimately, the directors of any large organization have to be judged not only by their own decisions but by the people they select to execute those decisions. In Harry Freeman, HAP's commissioners found a man who was intellectually able, a talented organizer, an accurate record keeper—a man who handled people well and did a dedicated job, his attempts to squash criticism of the operation when possible (not an entirely undesirable quality for an administrator) notwithstanding. However, any attempts to blunt criticism did not extend to the keeping of HAP historical records. Freeman's retention of the total story is responsible for whatever merit this study has. His selection of top subordinates, in a period of manpower scarcity, was acute. Those of his associates this author contacted remember him with respect, including his staff, his employers, and others connected with Vanport. He was a man of human sympathies. Following the flood he sent warm letters to those who contributed relief funds. The letters were tailored to each individual and frequently included a special touch, such as a book of flood pictures to a classroom of students in Alden, New York.

Some criticisms of HAP administration must be made, but in the total picture these are relatively minor. As noted, Vanport initially received a great deal of favorable local and national publicity, and HAP basked in its pleasant glow. When Vanport's public image began to reverse, it took great pains to suppress unfavorable publicity. The commissioners were, like the officers of most administrative bodies, quite sensitive to criticism and preferred to operate out of the public eye as much as possible. Early in 1943 they debated over whether the minutes of commissioners' meetings were open to the public. Their attorney advised them that they probably were open, but no one could just enter the office and review them; permission would have to be requested. Eventually, regular attendance of HAP meetings by an *Oregonian* reporter made any secrecy difficult. In the usual bureaucratic manner HAP attempted to control published employee statements by requiring any employee first to submit any scheduled comments to the administration. This sensitivity to criticism remained throughout the history of Vanport, as evidenced by the commissioners' decision to suspend publication of the Vanport *Tribune* due to its occasionally hostile stance on HAP policy.[88]

When employee negligence caused problems, the

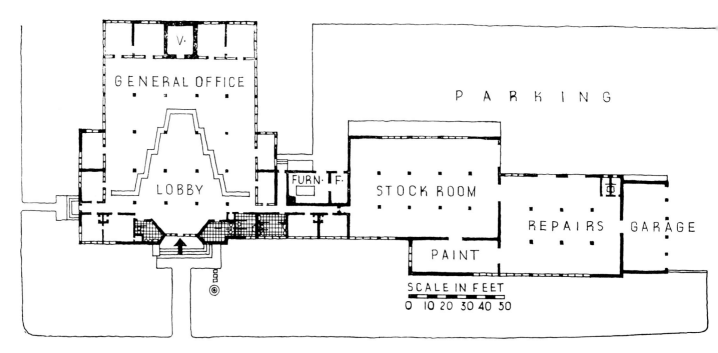

Floor plan for the administration building. (*Architectural Forum*, August 1943)

administration was not very eager to admit its responsibility. In one case a tenant's apartment was burglarized after a HAP worker entered it and left it open. When HAP's attorney informed the administrators they were legally at fault, their response was—make him sue, otherwise the Authority would be inundated with claims.[89]

The Housing Authority made an overwhelming effort to give taxpayers their money's worth, attempting to keep salaries and expenses down, and to cut overtime. Operating costs were largely kept within project income. As tenancy declined the commissioners insisted on personnel reductions. When the Vancouver, Washington Authority suggested HAP send 43 employees to a Spokane, Washington meeting of the National Association of Housing Officials, the request was considered completely out of line, and only nine were authorized to attend. Rigid control of lessees was maintained, proper

records and auditing procedures insisted upon. There were constant complaints of HAP fees being too high, that profit making was difficult. Business bonanzas were scarce, an unusual situation in the history of United States business-government partnerships. The Housing Authority even tried to get Multnomah County to pay for property damage done to apartments in Vanport by the county's welfare cases—the welfare department refused.[90]

Commissioners spent considerable time on housing authority business, a major part of which was concerned with Vanport City. After the flood, meeting agendas tailed off drastically, but much of the remaining business dealt with problems revolving around Vanport refugees. This time was willingly donated as a public service, in radical contrast to Vanport residents who, at least during the war years, could seldom be prevailed upon to render any voluntary public service. Time demands were so heavy, in fact, that at one point HAP inquired of FPHA about the possibility of some compensation for the commissioners. The reply was: Kentucky and Massachusetts laws permitted it, but California had turned it down; FPHA did not recommended it. No further follow-up effort was made.[91]

The Housing Authority of Portland took some innovative actions at Vanport. In March 1943, early in the project's history and at the peak of war production, HAP originated the idea of setting aside 56 family units for temporarily housing transient workers' families until permanent housing could be obtained. In December 1945, Harry Freeman established a separate section for veterans at Vanport in an effort to counteract local prejudices and convince them to try the housing. Thus began Vanport's famous "Veterans' Village." When Dr. S.E. Epler proposed locating an extension center of the Oregon State System of Higher Education in Vanport, Freeman and the Board of Commissioners immediately sensed the value of the suggestion and worked hard to help make it the success it eventually became.[92]

COMMUNITY INVOLVEMENT

Although in their early study of tenant instability at Vanport, Kilbourn and Lantis concluded that the administration functioned mainly as the operator of a furnished apartment agency, subsequent developments showed this to be much too harsh a judgment. Though one might disagree with its "big brother" attitude towards beer parlors, gambling, vice, and whether the hoped for improved morality occurred, HAP's concern

Street scene near the administration building in Vanport. Aside from the shipyards, this building was really the nerve center of Vanport. (OHS neg. 68785)

for the inhabitants of Vanport City was genuine. The commissioners considered securing a public relations man to instruct Vanport employees on the necessity of greater courtesy. Areas next to the project were set aside for victory gardens, a probably hopeless undertaking considering their availability for juvenile depredation. But the most telling evidence of their concern was their refusal to abandon responsibility for Vanport's residents after the flood. They worked hard to find trailers for housing, and when the physical deficiencies of the trailer village became apparent, they searched for better alternatives.[93]

The board of commissioners tried hard to develop a sense of community in Vanport and encourage citizen participation in the project's affairs, but to no avail. Perhaps they actually did not wish to relinquish control of the decision-making, and instead encouraged activity of an advisory nature, helpful in policy implementation. Nevertheless, commitment to the development of citizen participation must be credited to the board.

In May 1943, even before construction of the city was completed, the commissioners proposed the election of an advisory council. They envisaged dividing Vanport into districts each of which would elect a member to a kind of Vanport City Council, which would advise HAP. At subsequent meetings the commissioners regularly inquired as to what was being done to implement their suggestions. It soon appeared as if Manager J.L. Franzen, anticipating many difficulties, was stalling. A letter from the FPHA Regional Office did not exactly encourage the idea either, stating "past experience shows that when tenant government is initiated prematurely, such government tends to take upon itself responsibility for all sorts of functions which must rest with management." Furthermore, "the only people who emerge as leaders are those with some political axe to grind." The letter ended with the suggestion the whole thing be postponed until the tenants requested it.[94]

Reluctantly HAP switched to the possibility of an appointive advisory committee. Candidates could be submitted by various groups within the project, whose background would then be examined. To this suggestion Franzen replied that as yet no organized tenant groups existed. In August 1943 the management at Vanport City did make a half-hearted attempt to organize neighborhood councils. A few meetings were held, attended mainly by non-working women, and the topics shifted quickly to children's activities, handicrafts, story hours, and possible assistance to Cub and Boy Scout groups. One gathering demonstrated how to cook a 13 pound turkey in one of Vanport's 10 by 10 by 7 inch ovens, another how to use Oregon greens. Black citizens appeared to be the most active: they formed an interracial council and promoted the swing shift dance that led to Vanport's first real racial tension. However, the whole neighborhood council movement died rather quickly.[95]

During the wartime years all attempts to encourage citizen participation failed miserably. Whatever the reasons may have been, none could be assigned to the board of commissioners. Despite its aversion to criticism, the board was willing to try and break new ground, dedicated to the theory of participation. Every effort was expended to accomplish this goal, even to the extent of chastising its own administrative personnel, who could always find reasons it would not work. Manager J.L. Franzen in a December 1943 report, credited the tenants' lack of interest in taking part in their own government to the unfamiliar environment—a world of strangers temporarily mixed together. The attempt should be postponed. After all, he reasoned, it took five years to become oriented in a normal community. So the commissioners waited a couple of months before again inquiring about progress. This time Franzen replied that "common interests, neighborliness, hometown spirit" were slow in developing and should not be forced, but "gradually cultivated."[96]

58

Finally the commissioners gave up the effort. Perhaps Franzen and the others were right. An article by a Portland Realty Board member declared the people lacked civic spirit. Superintendent of Schools James T. Hamilton stated in 1945 that there was very little adult participation and every attempt to bring it about failed; that "Vanport is operated like a big hotel and community participation is about as successful as it would be in any large hotel." Later, when he was in the center of a broiling community controversy, he probably would have liked to revise the statement. Securing volunteers was extremely difficult. A meeting called to organize a Boy Scout program for the whole of Vanport drew only 57 people. The shortage of volunteers at the new Red Cross center led Meier and Frank Company (Portland's largest department store) to contribute a full page newspaper appeal for more help.[97]

The reasons for this dearth of community spirit might be found in Stanley Elkins' and Eric McKitrick's analysis of the development of democracy on different frontiers and its correlation with housing projects. They observed that people moving into a poorly planned project facing massive problems such as no schools, churches, electricity, community halls, grocery stores, adequate streets, criminal protection, or other city services were driven into participation. After being forced into action the participation became a form of self-expression and built common traditions. However, a well-planned, organized and operated project never elicited any such response. The pattern of a citizenry forced into participation due to lack of structure resembled the situation in settlements founded by pioneers who left New England to move West. In contrast, nothing of this nature happened in the South where the planters in their migration into Alabama and Mississippi created a less diversified society with fewer problems and provided the necessary government through the county court.[98] Vanport City, as a carefully planned

project, resembles the latter pattern of development. This may explain the difficulties encountered in the attempts to secure resident participation.

The situation that developed at Vanport following the war provides further support for such an interpretation. A sense of community began to emerge. In 1946 the federal government withdrew its school support and discontinued the summer school program. From this point on, educational financing became a major struggle. Seventy adults volunteered as recreation supervisors, and money for recreation supplies and equipment was raised. The citizens, aided by HAP, mounted a vigorous program (considered in more detail in the next chapter) to obtain further federal financing. Vanport students joined the attempt to influence legislation for funds to replace a junior high school destroyed by fire. By 1948 the number of people who bought telephone company stock in order to participate in the unique tax base elections jumped from 2 to 149. Property ownership was required for voting in the tax base elections. Because Vanport had no property owners other than the federal government, buying shares of telephone company stock made one an owner of the company's equipment, thus conferring the right to vote. This evolving community spirit was noted by the president of the executive council of the Vanport Parent-Teacher Clubs when, in the midst of the confrontation between citizens and school directors in February 1948, he declared that the interest aroused would serve as a basis for greater things in the future.[99]

PUBLIC VS. PRIVATE HOUSING

The veterans' colony, actively promoted by Harry Freeman, added to the sense of community. It became widely known as "Veterans' Village," an appellation used in a feature story in the Oregon *Journal Pacific Parade Magazine*. The article encouraged veteran housing in Vanport by arguing this was the way for returning G.I.s to beat the housing shortage if they could only "forget preconceived ideas and prejudices." Veterans began to respond. More and more buildings were prepared by HAP and added to the "village." Some of the women started to paint, tidy up and add little touches to the buildings and grounds. Some even began to like the accommodations in contrast to those of their former peripatetic army life. The ex-soldiers and their wives quickly became catalysts in disputes revolving around the public schools and Vanport Extension Center.[100]

What HAP had tried so diligently to promote finally developed from pressures exerted by the problems of school finance, veterans' housing, higher education, and racial issues (discussed in a following chapter). These common concerns led to that sense of community so long absent. Vanporters even began to participate in Portland area flower and vegetable garden and home beautification contests and started to defend Vanport against unsavory impressions of the town allegedly created by the Oregon *Journal* (a charge the newspaper took pains to deny).[101]

Shortly before the end of World War II HAP received an increasing barrage of public criticism for its supposedly anti-permanent public housing bias—a reputation largely stemming from confusing, vacillating, sometimes inconsistent shifts in federal policy, whose makers were groping with the new concept of a welfare state. The assault got underway in 1945 when a regional FPHA project planner publicly charged Portland and Seattle with "missing the boat" by not applying for postwar housing for low income groups. Chairman Moores replied that HAP was busy with managing 50 percent more housing than any other authority in the United States (New York City was second; Vancouver, Washington, third), and although trying to plan for the future, it could get no federal decisions on Vanport as a model industrial area, or on disposition of any of the other temporary projects. In addition, the figures cited in the charge had never been discussed with HAP or verified. Moores did request a deadline extension for submitting estimates of need.[102]

Shortly after the Vanport flood, Drew Pearson moved the attack to a national level, charging that most of the commissioners were dedicated to private housing, guilty of nepotism and arbitrary actions, and that a new board should be named. An Oregon *Journal* editorial reiterated the charges. The accusation distorted the real picture. The commissioners and the Authority were handed a temporary, wartime public housing job, prolongation of which obviously conflicted with the interests of private land development. Some commissioners did represent private development interests, since this was their only experience with property management. Nonetheless there is distinct evidence they were not operating solely to benefit private enterprise.[103]

United States Senator Harry Cain of Washington (who really represented the private housing point of view) introduced a bill that would have arbitrarily transferred all federal housing functions to FWA with instructions that FWA dispose of war housing by December 1948. The Housing Authority fought it vigorously. Many HAP officials, along with veterans and tenants, traveled to Seattle to see Senator Cain and to protest the legislation. Chairman Herbert J. Dahlke, appeared before a hearing of the Joint Committee on Housing held in Portland. He declared that HAP with its 13,000 living units was helping keep housing price inflation under control and enabling the estimated one-quarter of the 12,000 tenants who wanted to buy to wait for lower prices. Although believing that price competition would eventually solve the problem, Dahlke stated, that if the government insisted on liquidating the housing, HAP would like to buy it as a check on prices until better houses were built.[104]

During the years immediately following the Vanport

flood the attack continued, the federal government's welfare state position became solidified, and the composition of HAP underwent radical change. Although Herbert Dahlke would remain, and his wife would follow him onto the board of commissioners, the Vanport flood might be said to mark the end of one era and the transition to another. During the wartime years new and expanded governmental housing activity occurred. Enlisted into this service as HAP commissioners were several patriotic, dedicated men of great financial and administrative ability who served generously, ethically, and well. Coming from and representing private interests, they operated at a time when federal government control was not so fully established. As the emergency subsided, as governmental philosophy shifted to permanent public housing for low income groups, and as federal control was tightened these more individualistic directors tended to disappear; they were replaced by individuals less talented in the marketplace but more oriented to the developing conceptions of the welfare state.

SCHOOL

As with almost all aspects of Vanport life, the public school system was unique, differing greatly from practices of the time. It experimented in ways many local and state systems would later imitate. Because of these new approaches and Vanport's nationwide publicity value, it received much national attention. In February 1948, The Vanport *Tribune* reported that a committee of United States Congressmen ranked the system in the country's top 30.[1] With its nursery schools, summer sessions, and extended day-care it committed the federal government to 24-hour responsibility for many Vanport children.

Superintendent James T. Hamilton argued successfully and persuasively for the replacement of parental responsibilities with school facilities. Scouting and other youth groups could not obtain leaders. The combination of restricted living quarters, weather, and parents working different or non-day shifts simply forced the children outside beyond locked doors, and into delinquency and gang formation. Conscientious parents were leaving vital wartime jobs and returning to their former residences because of these conditions. In Vanport's time-disoriented life, mores and traditions of previous communities no longer prevailed, and it was impossible to conduct wholesome children's activities within the home. Hamilton maintained parental cooperation was almost non-existent.[2]

The very first school planning called for educational responsibility to be taken over by the Portland school district. Secret meetings were held between the board of education and representatives from the Office of Education. Finally, in a public meeting the board voted to assume control, with two directors in opposition. The U.S. Office insisted that all district funds be spent before the Vanport deficit was figured, including previously delinquent tax collections. When further complications arose over the question of state law in regards to a district operating outside its boundaries the board rescinded its action, leaving the U.S. Office of Education to search elsewhere.[3]

A school contract was then worked out with a nearby small local district, Columbia School District Number 33. It had a total of six teachers and 150 students. After a set of elaborate negotiations the contract was signed between the Housing Authority of Portland representing the Federal Public Housing Administration and the district. This tiny district was now to handle an expanded school program for a community of nearly 40,000. The Federal Public Housing Administration was to negotiate each year with Federal Works Administration for the necessary funds. If the district experienced a shortage at the end of the year the amount, if approved, would be made up by in-lieu-of-tax payments. The expected first year cost was $500,000. This

Superintendent of Vanport schools, James T. Hamilton. (Courtesy of Reed College archives)

ornamented with brick veneer, one of the few uses of brick in Vanport. They contained 12 classrooms, a kindergarten, library, office, gymnasium, and an assembly hall separate from the gymnasium. The child-care centers or nursery schools were constructed from a stock plan furnished by a government agency in Washington, D.C., and no changes were permitted. As a result much bureaucratic paperwork was needed to effect some very necessary revisions. More school facilities were added at a later date.[5]

The school buildings opened as they were completed, the first in March 1943 and the last in July. In the interim it was necessary to press apartment buildings into school service. The five elementary schools could handle up to 5,000 students on a double shift basis, an arrangement which federal authorities insisted upon and to which Superintendent Hamilton vigorously dissented, continually appealing for more buildings. When the war was over the double shift was finally abandoned. Original nursery school capacity was about 1,000 and there was always a surplus of these facilities, while the elementary schools were still full in early 1945. High school students were bused to either Portland's Roosevelt or Jefferson High, and tuition paid. If the student provided his own transportation (difficult under wartime conditions) any Portland high school could be attended. In 1945, during one of the periods of Vanport's peak occupancy, there were only 750 of these, another indicator of the unusual youth of Vanport parents.[6]

To run this 12-month, double shifted, extended day school and nursery operation, a superintendent and a staff of about 230 were assembled. By today's standards the overall student-teacher ratio of 30 to 1 seems high, but at that time it appeared to be adequate. In mid-December of 1942 a search was instituted by Columbia School District Number 33 for a suitable superintendent. Ten applicants took a civil service examination held at the Multnomah County Courthouse. Nine of the 10 were from Oregon. Oral interviews by a large com-

basic organizational structure was modified in 1944 when a new district was created for Vanport and East Vanport, named Vanport District Number 33, while the old Columbia District became Number 2.[4]

Construction began early in 1943 on five elementary and six nursery schools, located in two school centers. Grades seven and eight were not split between the two centers, all being located in Center Number 1. The elementary buildings were L-shaped, one-story frame, and

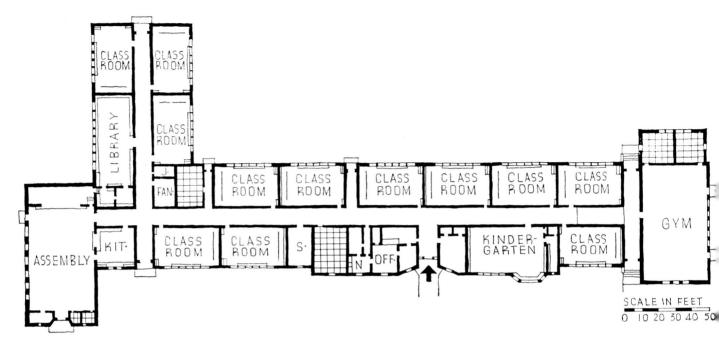

Lay-out for a typical elementary school in Vanport. (*Architectural Forum*, August 1943)

mittee that included the state superintendent and the Columbia District School Board followed the written test. James T. Hamilton, a former superintendent of the Newberg, Oregon schools and an assistant professor at Portland's Reed College, was selected.[7]

Despite the wartime teacher shortage there were 350 applicants for the first group of 133 jobs of a professional nature. Surprisingly, almost all were from Oregon (only 25 from Washington, five from Idaho, and two from Nevada). They too, were given written examinations. The examinations were graded at Oregon College of Education, and 120 teachers, two principals, three vice-principals, three supervisors, three school nurses, a dental nurse, and a director of research were selected. Teachers were employed on a 12-month basis with only a two week vacation. It was some time before they realized they were actually being paid less than

other area teachers on a per time basis. In addition they had to work a six day, 44-hour week and were allowed no credit for service before coming to Vanport. Salaries did not become roughly equalized with other Oregon first class districts until the 1945–46 school year when summer operations were discontinued. At that time elementary school averages for both were slightly over $2,000, while the top at Vanport for those who possessed Master's degrees and had been at Vanport since the beginning was $250 per month for nine and one quarter months. State of Oregon teaching certificates were required, either standard or temporary ones. Housing the teachers became a critical problem and was only solved when in-migrant teachers (those not already living in the Portland area) were declared eligible for Vanport housing.[8]

In opening the schools the district encountered the

usual problem of late equipment arrival for the buildings. This was compounded by the bureaucratic problems inherent in the federal financing. But by far the largest early administrative problem connected with the school plant was the divided responsibility. In the original lease between HAP (representing FPHA) and Columbia District Number 33, operation and maintenance of the buildings was assigned to HAP. Thus, HAP furnished heat, electricity, water, and janitorial services in addition to upkeep. Immediately problems arose over who was to pay for repairs occasioned by things not done or improperly done during the construction period.[9]

As the custodian of the buildings, HAP took over the scheduling of use during non-school hours, to which the school administration quickly took exception, and it also assigned groups for the evening hours. The result was many complaints from churches when they found their space pre-empted. In arguing their case the school board maintained that under Oregon law the responsibility belonged to them, and if it had known what the situation would be it would not have taken over the school operation. The board applied directly to FWA for additional funds to handle maintenance and operation. The Housing Authority of Portland gave way, adopting a policy of leasing the buildings to the district with complete jurisdiction going to the schools. It soon refused even to furnish maintenance men on a reimbursible basis as the school district paid a lower wage scale. Thus the only connection that remained was HAP operation of furnaces in the recreation buildings, furnaces that also heated the schools, and the schools were billed for heat, as they were for water and electricity. So from the beginning of 1944 on, the paths of the school district and HAP almost never crossed except for one "tem-

Original 1944 caption: "For mother and father a day of work . . . for the children a day of fun and growth." (OHS neg. 78701)

All children went through consultation interviews for placement in the right grade-level or day-care group. (OHS neg. 78702)

pest in a teapot," and it would be HAP that would later step into a bitter school-community dispute and in effect save the school administration.[10]

The school program that went into operation in 1943 may not have been, as a later resident handbook described it, ". . . the finest to be found anywhere,"[11] especially in its curriculum offerings, but the range and extent of its supplementary services provided a model that can hardly be matched anywhere today. And when

the federal largesse that made it possible was withdrawn with the slackening of the war emergency, Vanport residents finally realized the ride they had been on and hated to see it stop.

Residents were notified that Oregon law required all children between six and 16 years of age to be in school, unless the eighth grade had been completed. New arrivals to the schools were observed by a friendly teacher for a week and then assigned to a classroom group best

66

suited to the child's individual requirements. Basic class offerings followed standard Oregon practice, limited somewhat by the double shift, but there were kindergartens, not a common offering in many Oregon districts. Facilities were lacking for "manual training" or "domestic science," so little was offered. Superintendent Hamilton did secure three apartments from the Vanport management for some homemaking instruction. He felt it was particularly necessary because of the habit of many Vanport parents of leaving 10 and 11 year-olds at home to do the housework while they were away at their wartime jobs.[12]

An important part of the regular school program was its extended day operation. Six to 12 year-old children of working mothers could be brought to school as early as 5:45 A.M. when the first special teachers went to work. These teachers also instructed during the morning school sessions, while another group conducted

Snack carts were always a welcome sight. (OHS neg. 78696)

afternoon classes and stayed till 6:30. Breakfast was served in the cafeteria at 7:30, the children attended morning classes and stayed on into the afternoon until picked up, which could be closing time. Other children came later in the morning, ate lunch, went to afternoon classes, and could remain until 6:30. Twice a day snack wagons went through the schools, providing fruit, crackers, and ice cream bars. The child could be left under school care seven days a week, holidays included (if the shipyards were operating). Twelve percent of all Vanport children were on extended day-care, leading Superintendent Hamilton to appeal for more facilities.[13]

A full school program operated during the summer. Attendance was not required but ran at 60 percent. Five week sessions were followed by a week of vacation. In addition a Vanport Schools' children's summer camp was held at Nahcotta on Washington's Willapa Bay. Children could attend any one of the three weekly sessions for $14 plus a small transportation fee. For this they received all their meals, a varied activity program, and 24-hour-a-day supervision by counselors from the Vanport school district.[14]

Then there were the nursery schools or, more euphemistically, the Child Service Centers. They opened in the summer of 1943, operated on a 24-hour basis seven days a week, and employed mothers left their children for a very modest cost that covered little of the actual expense. Regulations were soon relaxed so that if only one parent was working but had to sleep during the day the children could still be brought. Two to twelve year-olds were taken at a night center, supper was provided along with sleeping facilities, then breakfast in the morning. The charge was $4.50 per week. At the day centers it was $3.00 per week, and one meal was served. Between the two, 24-hour care of a family's children was possible. One hundred fifty teachers conducted the operation. The Child Service Centers even provided a special service for cases of mild illness. If the child was brought

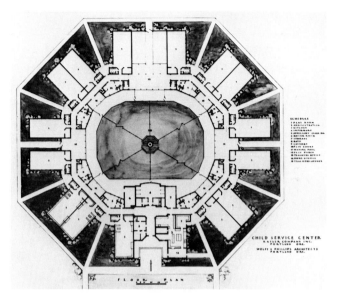

Architectural plans for Child Service Center. Wolff & Phillips architects. (OHS neg. 78699)

to a center, it would arrange for 24-hour day-care in the Vanport Hospital for $2.00 a day.[15]

These services represented quite a subsidy to Vanport citizens because they paid no direct school taxes during the first years and project rents certainly did not cover these costs. It was justified by Superintendent Hamilton, in a bulletin for residents, with the statement that in wartime parents are not able to do as much for their children, while still another public school publication declared, "No child need become a war casualty if both parents work." However, this reasoning apparently did not apply to the homeowner who also worked in the shipyard.[16]

Reports were current in January 1946 that federal support of the nursery school program would be discontinued now that the war was over. The center, located in the newly developing "Veterans' Village," was naturally quite popular, and rumors of closure led to some correspondence to HAP from veterans, who deplored such a possibility. As is often the case with such rumors, they quickly turned out to be correct. Harry Freeman tried to reassure the veterans that an attempt would be made to continue operation. Superintendent Hamilton stated the Columbia School District could not furnish any money. It was continued for a short while with Community Chest funds, with maintenance contributed by HAP, and then the unusual service finally ceased.[17]

Ever since the regular school program began in 1943, Superintendent James T. Hamilton had continually appealed, in the name of the children, for an end to the double shift. His entreaties fell upon deaf ears until 1945. Federal officials who had private knowledge of

A snack time break at the Child Service Center. (OHS neg. 78698)

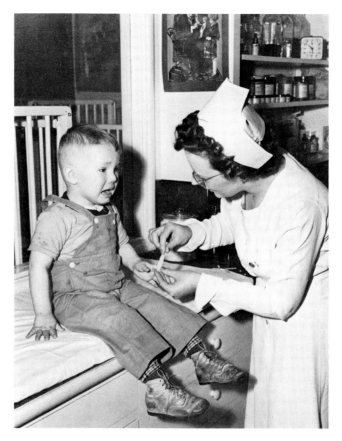

The Child Service Centers always had a nurse on hand to take care of the day's accidents. (OHS neg. 78697)

how well the war in the Pacific was going and who knew of the coming phase-out of shipyard contracts withdrew their objections. Full-time school operations started in September 1945. The agreement stipulated a class average load of 30 must be maintained, and as Vanport's population declined and some facilities became unnecessary, they had to be closed.[18]

During early 1946 Vanport citizens had to face their first critical problem. It called forth the first real outpouring of civic spirit, and from this time on school

Aerial view of Swan Island Child Service Center. (OHS neg. 78700)

crises dominated the life of Vanport, along with racial issues, marking a considerable change from the apathetic, halcyon, wartime days. Not only did the nursery schools face the loss of federal funds, but there was the distinct possibility of all Lanham Act moneys for deficit school financing being terminated at the end of the 1945–46 school year in June. Oregon senators and representatives were hurriedly contacted. They succeeded in obtaining informal assurances from powerful congressional committee members that some moneys would eventually be forthcoming in some form or other. However, there was to be no more summer school, and Vanporters found out for the first time what it was like to have 6,000 unoccupied children roaming Vanport's small area, a problem previously solved through federal beneficence.[19]

The amount of government subsidy was finally determined in a more traditional fashion. A millage rate to be applied to Vanport's property valuation had to be established by Oregon voters under provisions of state law. Residency and property ownership were required for the franchise in this case, but there were no Oregon property owners in Vanport, just the federal government. The problem was solved in a very unusual manner. A one voter district for all Vanport was created when Miss Laura Kellar, one of the school principals and a resident of Vanport City, bought a share of telephone company stock, making her an owner of the company's equipment. A duly advertised election was held to establish a fifty mill tax rate, which, when applied to the federal property valuation would yield a $300,000 in-lieu-of-tax payment. The vote was one to zero, and

Lanham Act funds again provided the money. However, this sum did involve some belt-tightening and was a supplement to other financing from Oregon state sources. Churches using school buildings were now required to pay for heat and custodial services during periods when these would not ordinarily be available. Thus another fringe benefit from Vanport's lush period disappeared.[20]

The Housing Authority began doling out the money. There were questions as to which funds (federal or state) should remain for last use. Harry Freeman's more careful accounting procedures were in sharp contrast to the rather loose school board practices. Previously, HAP had resolved any disputes or problems amicably and helpfully. In addition to giving way on the control of after school use it had come up with money to rescue the school district when the schools incorrectly placed funds from FPHA in their budget instead of requesting all monies from FWA. Now HAP started to scrutinize more carefully the financial operations of the district, and a serious disagreement over a relatively minor matter soon arose.[21]

It became evident to HAP that the schools had not paid several thousand dollars in utility bills owed to HAP. The board of commissioners, always sticklers for proper financial operation, set out to collect. Because of their faulty bookkeeping practices, the school district at first believed it did not owe the money. It became quite irate, charging HAP with attempted usurpation of authority and collection of unauthorized claims. Finally, driven to admit the validity of the bill, and by implication their poor record maintenance, the district declared it could not pay a previous year's budget item out of the current year's budget, and demanded HAP pay the full amount of the bill and include it in the next year's budget. If HAP did not wish to do this the school district would sue HAP, and furthermore it challenged

HAP to sue them for the money. The Housing Authority was against any carryover because of the possibility of city or county control of school operations during the following year.[22]

To Harry Freeman and the board of commissioners the issue became one of principle, and they proceeded to set up the schedule for the remaining in-lieu-of-tax payments so that the sum due was deducted. Superintendent Hamilton appealed to Freeman's superior in FPHA, who admitted to some "personal confusion" over the problem, a state of being that Freeman would have assigned to him as a permanent characteristic. Eventually, FPHA forced HAP to make the payment. Harry Freeman may have contemplated a little revenge as he proceeded to assemble the inventory of federal property loaned to the school district. However, other instincts prevailed, and that fall he set HAP on a course that, it might be said, helped preserve the job of Superintendent Hamilton.[23]

Federal efforts to withdraw funding continued. In January 1947, FPHA notified HAP that no supplemental money would be available for the school year starting the following September. All financing must come from local and state sources, instead of the previous approximately 50 percent. The previous year's drama was replayed, federal authorities eventually gave in, and another election was held. This time the vote was two to zero and established the millage on which the federal government would base its in-lieu-of-tax payments. The millage was four times greater than that of nearby Portland. A third election in the early spring of 1948, in anticipation of the following school year, produced an amazing result. While everyone expected the usual one or two vote election, 149 turned out to cast affirmative ballots. They had quietly bought Pacific Telephone or Portland General Electric stock. It was another indication of Vanport's rising community consciousness.[24]

As the fall of 1947 approached, Vanport City's population had stabilized in the 18,000 vicinity, and its school system was down to four schools with an expected enrollment of approximately 2,500. The year was not to open quietly. A crisis developed that brought forth the greatest community participation Vanport was ever to experience, and best illustrated the arguments of professors Elkins and McKitrick on how local democracy was produced.[25]

A controversy the previous year between the public schools and newly emerging Vanport College over school building use (in which the college did not get its way) planted the seeds that sprouted into a raging dispute. Afterwards a residue of bitterness remained, especially amongst Vanport veterans attending the college. In a quiet maneuver in the early summer of 1947, veterans and other college students living in Vanport turned out in sufficient numbers to elect two students to the school board (William McLeod and Herman Zukerman), while other residents unaware of what was happening remained at home. Apparently the veterans/students were out to wreak vengeance on Superintendent Hamilton, and another newly elected member of the board (Edward Perkins) shared their point of view, giving the group a majority of the five members.[26]

Superintendent Hamilton did not passively sit by, but organized his own attack. Vanport businessman Edward Perkins was declared ineligible for his board seat because of non-attendance at meetings, being replaced by his runner-up in the election. The ethics committee of the Oregon Education Association found "insoluble conflicts" present on the board and recommended McLeod resign. Hamilton charged, by implication, that the two students' motive was revenge and stated, for publication, ". . . men of greater discernment and moral judgment would have resigned." But the two directors stood their ground. Then Hamilton, with the active support of the Vanport Education Association (teachers), an-

nounced the schools would not open as scheduled unless McLeod and Zukerman resigned. It was not supposed to be a strike, merely a postponement. McLeod charged Hamilton with thwarting the "will of the voters." The dissident directors suggested it was the duty of all to get on with the business of educating children, while the assistant director of Vanport City College stated the previous year's disagreement had been settled satisfactorily, and there was no ill will towards Superintendent Hamilton.[27]

At this point HAP, feeling its overall responsibility for operation of the project, demanded that the schools be opened as scheduled and appointed a committee of competent, disinterested citizens to investigate the controversy. Hamilton gave way, and the schools started as scheduled. Both warring factions submitted acceptances to the investigating committee, the board members requesting that rumors and unsupported complaints be kept out and that the investigators confine themselves to whether the board or superintendent had done anything detrimental to the public schools. The power alignment was further confused as the state Attorney General upheld Perkins' removal, while his replacement had to resign from the board in order to keep his post office job (Hatch Act).[28]

Another proposal was advanced by the American Veterans' Committee (AVC). All the directors should resign and a new election be held. The AVC declared the veterans were not solely seeking control but were fighting for democratic participation, and supported the three directors in their refusal to resign. Its suggestion was disregarded.[29]

The inquiry committee selected by HAP was indeed a prestigious one. Chaired by David B. Simpson, a former president of the Portland Chamber of Commerce, it included Rupert R. Bullivant, former president of the Oregon State Bar Association; M.E. Steele, member of the Executive Board of the Oregon State Federation of

Labor; Mrs. I.E. Hervin, former president of the Portland League of Women Voters; and Dr. Ray S. Dunn, pastor of the Rose City Methodist Church.[30]

The committee did its work well. At the 16 October board of commissioners' meeting, they were ready to put the report into the record. First of all they recommended release of the report to the press and that all interested parties be supplied with copies. Following this came the findings. The committee felt that the school directors' stated reservations had hampered its investigation. It had decided not to publish the various allegations that had been hurled, the ". . . bickering, rumors, wounded feelings, charges, countercharges, suspicions, and threats . . . which all participants should be pleased to have quietly ended and hidden discreetly from public attention." The report lauded the Vanport school system, but also declared there were no legal grounds to prevent the three directors from holding office.[31]

More specific findings were: the three directors exercised poor judgment in criticizing the superintendent, but they had the legal right to do so; Hamilton used poor administrative technique in refusing to explain the basis of actions challenged by the board, and in not attempting to work with the three directors; and both the superintendent and the staff used poor judgment in failing to understand their public responsibilities when they threatened not to open the schools unless one or all three of the directors resigned. This threat was inexcusable. Each of the parties was at fault, but the dispute was not so serious as to be irreconcilable. All were men of good character and could work together if they wished to do so. Consequently a meeting of the parties had been held, and they had agreed on this course. Whether they would work together could only be determined by time.[32]

Finally, the report concluded with a recommendation that the district look forward to union with Portland School District Number 1. A 1943 law passed by the Oregon State Legislature now made this possible. The three directors favored it, and Hamilton said he would cooperate in trying to achieve it. This was attempted but the Portland board did not want additional problems.[33]

At the meeting Hamilton made a statement which smacked a little of "sour grapes." He thanked the commissioners, but was dubious of the results of their actions, declaring the ". . . group that put the 'small men' in are out for control . . . ," and they were apt to get it by adding one of them to succeed Chairman Merald Simpson who was resigning from the board because of a possible job change that would make him ineligible.[34] It was democracy in action, and it would turn out that the forces backing Hamilton were able to exert enough pressure for him to win.

Early in 1948 Hamilton let it be known that he would probably resign at the end of the school year. This provided the opportunity for his supporters to organize a huge testimonial. At a night meeting in mid-February he was presented with a 95-foot long petition begging him to stay. It contained the names of 3,000 parents and supporters. Various dignitaries praised the superintendent, including Harry Freeman and Edwin C. Berry, executive secretary of the Urban League.

Final culmination of the dispute occurred at a noisy school board meeting on the evening of 24 February. William McLeod moved that Hamilton not be rehired for the following year. The large crowd's reaction was so intense that the evening closed with McLeod and Zukerman resigning. Only a few college students and AVC members supported them. Through necessity and conflict, community participation had finally arrived. As one Vanporter expressed it, "the next time we will get out and vote in the election." Superintendent Hamilton looked forward to another year.[35] On Sunday 30 May, all school problems disappeared as the flood waters inundated Vanport.[36]

Vanport's large school system, located wholly within

a federal housing project, offered an opportunity for re-definition of federal-state relationships in the field of education. Perhaps because of more essential wartime priorities, the federal government chose to ignore the possibilities and simply supplied the funds to a traditionally organized Oregon school district. It did supply a plan that carried within it concepts of nursery school and extended day-care, ideas that would not be very rapidly extended after the wartime emergency. Some traces of this expansive educational philosophy have only recently emerged (programs for the handicapped, Head-start, breakfasts) and financial pressures may hinder any further expansion. However, the wartime experience, not only in Vanport but in other war-swollen communities, helped pave the way for later massive injections of federal money into the regular school systems of the states in order to meet what were regarded as new crises such as competition with the U.S.S.R. and education of minorities.

In Superintendent James T. Hamilton, the Vanport School District possessed a man who believed in adding further sociological objectives to the schools. Whenever the family failed, the school should take up the slack. He worked hard and diligently for an expanded program, and while the federal government was freely providing the money, the range of school services could hardly be matched anywhere in the United States. He was able to operate the school district with a much greater degree of freedom than HAP could exercise in the administration of other aspects of the project. After much of the extra federal support was withdrawn, and many programs eliminated, he continued fighting for what he considered to be of paramount importance, his concept of the interests of the children.

VANPORT CITY COLLEGE

One of the few remaining tangible links to Vanport is Oregon's major urban collegiate institution, Portland State University. Had it not been for the unusual combination of circumstances present at Vanport City, the college would have been located elsewhere in the state, if created at all.

As previously noted, when the war ended and ship-yard activity wound down, large numbers of people left Vanport. In spite of the housing shortage, Vanport's image was so unfavorable that much of the housing went unoccupied. Harry Freeman set out to create and promote a separate veteran's area, and by early 1946 the "Veterans' Village" was successfully established. Many of these veterans planned to enroll in Oregon's colleges and universities under provisions of the "G.I. Bill." Anticipating this, the Oregon State System of Higher Education (OSSHE) employed Stephen E. Epler to act as a counselor to the Vanport veterans, and he took up residence there.[37]

The idea of bringing a lower division extension college to the veterans, to deflect the scramble for the totally inadequate living quarters in the existing college areas, has been credited to Epler in most sources. A story in the Portland *Oregonian* laid the idea's genesis to a golf game between Epler and Henry E. Stevens, assistant director of the General Extension Division of OSSHE. Originally it was intended as a temporary expedient. Stevens discussed the idea with Dean F.J. Cramer of the General Extension Division, who liked the proposal and decided to present it to the OSSHE Board. Meanwhile Epler called Harry Freeman, inquiring about the possible use of some of the Vanport buildings.[38]

The whole concept could never have gotten off the ground without the strong, active response of Harry Freeman. Instantly sensing the possibilities, he mailed his approval in an official letter to Epler on 14 February 1946 and the same day called FPHA Regional Director Jesse Epstein, following the call with a letter outlining the following points: housing was not available at Eugene, classes could be held night and day, there might

Vanport Extension Center brought a lower division extension college to the Portland area with the added bonus of abundant living quarters for veterans and their families. It evolved into Portland State University. (OHS neg. 58857)

eventually be 1,000 students, and HAP looked with great favor on the proposal. Freeman notified Epler the next day that he had secured verbal permission to go ahead.[39]

The idea originally met a cool reception from OSSHE, which at that moment was more interested in using a military installation at Klamath Falls. By mid-March, however, it decided to try a Vanport summer session, and if this proved successful, would consider the possibility of a winter operation. The Housing Authority quickly approved the proposal.[40] Stephen Epler, the 36 year-old navy veteran-turned-counselor, was selected to lead the new educational venture. Like so much of Vanport he was colorful and newsworthy. A *Time* magazine article, accompanied by a sizable photograph, featured "Ideaman" Epler's Vanport activities. Already known for his invention of six-man football, he was now credited with reviving a dying Vanport and persuading 17 vacationing professors to teach the summer session. Certainly, the national publicity that Vanport College (officially Vanport Extension Center) received aided the instructional talent search during a time of shortage, and helped secure prominent individuals like librarian Dr. Jean Black and Dr. C.A. Hubbard (famous for his bubonic plague work).[41]

By the time the summer session opened OSSHE had been sold on the idea of a college at Vanport. It dropped consideration of Klamath Falls, made the summer session a regular term, and prepared plans for fall continuance. A brochure outlined to veterans and others the advantages of Vanport Center College. A full-fledged part of OSSHE, and with comparable course numbers and outlines, it provided a first year of work fully transferable to the other state institutions. Engineering, pre-law, business administration, pre-med, pre-dental, and some liberal arts courses were offered. The newly created "Veterans' Village" furnished completely repaired, repainted apartment units renting from $30 to $49.50 per month, including all utilities, and veterans were sometimes eligible for even lower rates. The public/nursery school combination in Vanport allowed both parents to work or attend college, with the Child Service Center providing all day-care in the summer. In addition, there were all of Vanport's regular community services.[42]

The summer session's first-day enrollment was overwhelmingly masculine—151 men, 12 women. Eventually it rose to 221, although the number of women dropped to eight. Ninety-four percent were veterans. Fourteen of the courses resulted from student requests. The Oregon State System of Higher Education regarded the venture as a great success and on 26 July 1946 requested an indefinite lease. However, it sent the request to the National Housing Authority, instead of HAP or even FPHA, and it was promptly buried. Anticipating a fall enrollment of about 500, by late August OSSHE had received 1,200 applications (90 percent from veterans), and they were continuing to come in at the rate of approximately 200 per week. In desperation, OSSHE dispatched a letter to FPHA asking it to hurry the lease. The Federal Public Housing Authority moved into the breach, contacting HAP and Harry Freeman. Responding with vigor, HAP, in its eagerness to accede to almost any request caused one of Vanport's racial confrontations.[43]

The college asked HAP to move tenants from one of the areas nearby so that disabled veterans could occupy the units and thus minimize their problems in getting to class. The section happened to be occupied by blacks who when given notice to move, appealed to the Urban League of Portland and the National Association for the Advancement of Colored People (NAACP). These organizations conducted an investigation, the upshot of which was that the forced relocation was stopped and OSSHE rescinded its request.[44]

As a result of the high veteran attendance at the summer session and the overwhelming number of fall term applications, Vanport College made a desperate attempt to expand facilities. This led to permanent bitterness between it and the public school system. With permission from the school district, public school buildings had been used during the summer session and the college hoped to obtain at least one of these permanently, in addition to the two nursery centers, recreation center, and shopping center they were authorized to use.[45] But Superintendent Hamilton felt the school was needed by public school children, and it was obvious he was not going to relinquish the building voluntarily. So Stephen Epler, undoubtedly believing the college's role in veterans' education should have priority, mounted a public relations campaign to attain his objective.

Both of the Portland area's major newspapers, The Oregonian and Oregon Journal, had given a great deal of publicity to Vanport College. Several daily and Sunday features had described its founding and summer success. Now they entered this controversy. In editorials on 29 August both urged Hamilton to give in, the Oregon Journal implying that he was wrong, while the Oregonian, although not placing the blame on Hamilton, mentioned the college's lease problems and concluded Hamilton should accede in order that the college might open for the fall term.

Under pressure, Hamilton did not surrender. When OSSHE and HAP intervened, he called a public fact-finding meeting with the FPHA area supervisor presiding. The superintendent opened with a statement condemning the "irresponsible high pressure methods and the distortions of facts" contained in Vanport College's news releases and declared the Vanport School Board would no longer deal with the college. He proceeded to support his case. One college release, alleging that the public schools did not need Roosevelt School, stated that at one time there were 6,800 public school children, but that the enrollment had now dropped to 2,300. The former figure was really a cumulative total; the daily average attendance had been only approximately 4,000 at its peak, and this was when the double shift was in operation, with recreation halls also pressed into service. While using a cumulative figure for the high total, the college shifted to the lowest weekly average ever reached for its figure of 2,300. Superintendent Hamilton then showed clearly that the school facilities had been expressly promised only for the summer and produced letters proving Epler had been attempting to get Congressman Homer T. Angell and Senator Wayne Morse to exert pressure on District 33.[46]

The newspapers had anticipated a colorful battle between Hamilton and Epler. Both were certainly dedicated to their jobs and organizations. But the Oregon Journal's "expected fireworks" did not materialize. Charles Byrne, chief executive officer of OSSHE simply ordered Epler not to read his statement. In a magnificent display of mediating talent, he got all the groups to sit down together and try to work out a solution, after first declaring OSSHE did not presume to tell District 33 how much space it needed, and that, after all, both of them were interested in the education of youth.[47]

A compromise was quickly worked out. Vanport College, which had wanted facilities for 2,000 now compromised on 1,200, and through extended day use, these could actually service up to 1,500 students. The

Celebrating Vanport College's first birthday, Dr. Stephen E. Epler (left), director of Vanport Extension Center and Don Newman (right), student, approve a design for the college's birthday cake submitted by Irwin McFadden (center), graphic artist. (OHS neg. 69464)

Federal Public Housing Administration furnished Nurseries 3 and 4, recreation building space, and Shopping Center 2. Hamilton offered use of the school administration offices, promised he would try to close Nursery 6 and close the public schools at 2:00 P.M., after which the college could use the rooms. The college opening date was delayed for two weeks in order to ready the facilities. It was an effective solution. Pre-enrollment reached 1,755, but colleges then did not collect advance fees, and "no shows" dropped the figure to

1,315 at the end of the first week. This eventually rose to 1,410, thus the 1,500 figure turned out to be ample.[48]

Vanport College embarked on its highly successful career. Typical of urban colleges, three-fourths of its students were from Multnomah County. Uncharacteristically, winter term enrollment rose above that of the fall. By the time of its first anniversary celebration, almost 2,000 students had begun their education. Ninety percent were veterans and half were married. The average student age was 23, a distinct rise, and indicative of later patterns of college attendance when a larger proportion of older students would be enrolled. Because of the space problems, classes ran from 7:30 A.M. to 10:00 P.M., also a portent of the future. The War Assets Administration furnished much of the college's available equipment at little or no cost.[49]

The library did not open until late December. Created out of the old shopping center near the railroad tracks, it would seat only 10 percent of the students instead of the recommended 30 percent. With its few books, and the trains thundering by, it would have been totally inadequate were it not for the nearby community libraries and indefinite loan privileges from the Oregon State Library.[50]

Vanport College infused new life into the city. Instead of stagnation and slow decay, a feeling of vitality and community began to take hold as the young veterans took action to solve problems. Vanport, the Portland *Oregonian* declared, was "taking on the look" of a small college town. As the Office of Price Administration collapsed in the fall of 1946, prices rose, and shortages persisted in Vanport stores. With limited funds and lacking transportation, a group of students under the leadership of the student council president formed a cooperative buying club. Goods were bought in case lots and distributed the following Saturday morning. Others, including faculty, wanted to join. Advance orders were expanded, and the surplus put on shelves. The coopera-

The Vanport Co-op. With the collapse of the Office of Price Administration, a group of students formed a cooperative buying club. It was an enormous success. (OHS neg. 58852)

tive hired a part-time manager, and volunteers did the rest. Originally located in the kitchen of Engineering Hall, the store soon moved to larger quarters in what had been HAP Yard Station 6, and operated five afternoons a week. One of its greatest volume items was canned milk for babies. Items like Karo syrup and shortening, which could not be obtained in Vanport stores, now became available. Soon textbooks were added.[51]

As enrollment continued to rise throughout the first year, facilities continued to expand, as they would throughout the college's life at Vanport. The Housing Authority willingly acceded to almost every request. When OSSHE could locate no buildings in the immediate area to meet one particular need, it requested permission to erect four Quonset huts; permission was quickly granted along with use of a heating unit for the Quonsets. Three persons who wished to provide cafeteria service to the college were granted a lease for Yard Station 6. Another nursery school building (with Hamil-

ton's approval), more heating units, and an athletic field were soon added to the college. A very few extremely small industrial operations had use of several apartment buildings in the college area, and at the college's request two of these were moved to different locations. Invariably the commissioners' vote for requests was unanimous, and HAP always worked hard to secure the necessary FPHA approval. As buildings were added, rental to OSSHE did not increase. The college bore only the remodeling cost.[52]

In spite of the difficulties encountered during the attempt to move black residents from some of the apartments wanted by Vanport College, the institution requested one particular building for office space which currently held black residents. The Housing Authority submitted the request to FPHA. It gave "reluctant" approval, but only if the occupants were willing to move, and Regional Supervisor Jesse Epstein, in a letter to Byrne, used the occasion to attack what he termed the segregated pattern of the local authority. However, his only stated objection was that the policy was costly, resulting in a vacancy loss.[53]

Vanport College's first year had been memorable. National publicity showered down on the unique veteran-college relationship, often making special reference to a study demonstrating that its veterans got higher grades than non-veterans at the start, and that the gap widened with each term. Married veterans did the best of all. Vanport was the forerunner of a trend soon to be demonstrated all over the country. It now offered two years of degree work and varsity sports, intramurals, clubs, and social programs, along with a weekly student publication, The Vanguard (now the newspaper of Portland State University). Engineering and business administration were the two most popular programs. College officials liked to argue that student fees more than covered costs.[54] This perhaps applied to direct costs, but did not take into account the federal contribution of buildings and equipment or some administrative services rendered by OSSHE.

Vanport College celebrated its successful first year with a commemoration day on 26 May 1947. Henry A. Wallace, the Progressive candidate for president, in Portland on a political tour, gave the feature address. Despite the convivial college-HAP relations, one of the commissioners refused to attend, writing to Stephen Epler that anyone who criticized our foreign policy and advocated giving billions to the Soviets should not be allowed to speak on United States government property. Nevertheless, it was a happy occasion. Total registration the first year had reached 1,924, and although the facilities were still regarded as temporary, nothing but continued growth during the next year was anticipated.[55]

In his first annual report Stephen Epler acknowledged the great debt the college owed to HAP, stating, "Without the excellent cooperation of the Housing Authority of Portland in providing both classroom buildings and housing for students, the college program of the Vanport Extension Center could not have been accomplished." Buildings had been released even when it was inconvenient and expensive. The entire Board of Commissioners and staff had "done everything possible to further the college program."[56]

This happy relationship was to continue to the very end. In July, Harry Freeman spoke at a college assembly, as HAP and Vanport College united in opposition to the Cain-Russell Bill which would allow the disposition of public housing. The college lease was cut from $10,500 plus utilities to $2,100 plus utilities, when Dean Francis Cramer explained the money had to come out of student fees. This was done in spite of the takeover of additional buildings. The lease fee became based on the percentage of veterans attending. Herbert Dahlke (Chairman of the Board of Commissioners) proudly invited the U.S. Senate committee conducting hearings on public housing in Portland that summer, to

Salvaging a Columbia Hall college sign. (OHS neg. 68991)

view the color film produced by HAP on the college's development.[57]

Vanport College's bright prospects continued throughout the 1947–48 school year. Approximately 1,500 students actually enrolled for the fall term, and about one-fourth of these lived in Vanport. With their families, the Vanport residents numbered over 1,000. The 119 women students, although still a small percentage, nevertheless represented a 60 percent increase over the previous year. Only 23 students were from minority groups (seven Chinese, eight Japanese, eight Negro). One-third of the college's young faculty (average age, 37 in the 1946–47 school year) also resided in Vanport. In April and May additional facilities were again requested.[58]

By April OSSHE was thinking in terms of a long-term future for Vanport College. Edgar W. Smith, chairman of the Board of Higher Education, told Vanport students the college would continue as long as enrollment showed a need for it and a high veterans attendance was expected for at least 10 to 12 years. A happy second an-

The spirit of Vanport College emerged from the flood waters in the form of Portland State University. (OHS neg. 68826)

niversary celebration held on 21 May culminated in a formal dance at Portland's venerable Multnomah Hotel; nothing but bright expectations lay on the horizon.[59] Nine days later the railroad grade behind the college crumbled, and its Vanport existence was pounded into oblivion by the tumbling, swirling waters.

The fact that housing for veterans was available at Vanport and not at Eugene led to a chain of events that eventually produced a major urban university in the state of Oregon. In the process, Vanport, for the first time, experienced something giving a sense of community identification, belonging, and pride. In addition a whole host of problems arose, problems that necessitated active participation if they were to be solved— makeshift classrooms, high prices, shortages of basic living commodities, the Cain-Russell Bill, and competition for classroom space. The necessity of participation created a vitality separate and distinct from the traditional institutional forms and caused a cleavage in operation of the democratic process between those housing projects with minor problems and smooth administration and those where the administrative authorities could not by themselves arrive at solutions.

Although Vanport College lives on in its transplanted form of Portland State University, it is impossible for this writer to leave the subject without at least a wistful, speculative mention of what might have been, had it not been for the flood. As the housing at Vanport decayed or was eventually razed and the need for collegiate facilities continued to grow, someone undoubtedly would have been struck with the realization of Vanport's potential as a magnificent campus. Its ideal size, its waterways and trees, and its easy access inevitably would have led to a campus community in the heart of a developing urban center.

80

CRIME AND DELINQUENCY

No massive set of social problems arose out of the Vanport experience. Indeed, social relations was the one area in which Vanport was not unique. Assimilation within the city was not difficult, and the prejudices existing in the greater urban area were abstract and general, not easily translated into specific, individual actions. Crime was present, but not in an amount or intensity to differentiate it greatly from the whole of Portland and Multnomah County. Juvenile vandalism did become a special problem because of Vanport's restricted size, concentrated population, and always present vacant buildings, which were a result of the excessive tenant turnover. When coupled with the nationwide acceleration of parental neglect, the situation offered unparalleled opportunity for destructiveness. The relatively high proportion of blacks (for the Portland area) did not create any really shattering problems although important steps were taken towards the acceptance of a greater number of non-whites within the Portland community.

Vanport's social stresses were not comparable to some of the other wartime industrial communities (such as those surrounding the Ford Motor Company bomber plant at Willow Run, Michigan) where social impacts were greater, and perhaps less lasting. Urban facilities were available and could handle the load with a little stretching and accommodation. Reasonably adequate housing was quickly constructed and efficiently operated. Transportation problems were satisfactorily solved. No really severe competition for facilities, recreation, or goods crystallized between "The Newcomers" and "Folks in Possession," such as that described by Lowell Carr and James Stermer in their study of Willow Run. When the shipyards closed, many of the in-migrants were quickly integrated, along with many who left only to return later. Their legacy was a larger metropolitan area, its pulse quickened by the economic stimulations of the war and by the youth of the migrants.[1]

Adult recreation remained somewhat of a problem throughout the city's life, even though the script on the back of one of Portland General Electric's paintings of life in Vanport stated ". . . the Housing Authority of Portland is meeting the recreational problems of the fast growing population with originality and understanding."[2] This certainly was true for the youth programs previously described, but only for the time when Lanham Act funds were available. However, the need for adult recreation was never successfully met, especially during the war years when gasoline rationing was in effect, although shipyard workers could usually manage an extra supply to take them out of Vanport for recreational purposes in Portland, Vancouver, or nearby Jantzen Beach.

The Housing Authority of Portland was cognizant of the problem, but between its solicitude for the morals of Vanport residents and the Federal Public Housing Authority's reluctance to allow expenditures for commercial recreational activities, little was ever done. Proposals for creating a commercial recreation center by moving a large, unused building from a Vancouver project, establishment of a bowling alley in another commercial building, and converting a closed nursery school into a lunch, card and billiard room were all rejected by FPHA. It seemed as if the only thing that could get consideration was something for children or young people. After first turning down a suggestion for a skating rink in one of the recreation centers because of the noise factor, HAP reconsidered and approved the request following appeals from the Parent Teacher Association, Project Services, and approval by FPHA.[3]

One of the strangest features of life in Vanport was the lack of a single outlet for "on premises" consumption of alcoholic beverages of any sort. This policy encountered difficulties after the war. With the formation of "Veterans' Village," one cafe operator reported to HAP that the veterans insisted on bringing their own beer into the establishment if it could not be purchased, and he requested permission to install a bar after securing the proper liquor commission license. The Housing Authority agreed, but FPHA disapproved. In a show of independence HAP decided to let its action stand, but in the end it had to accede. So to the end Vanport remained a large city where beer was sold only by the bottle for "off-premises" consumption.[4]

Throughout the project's life juvenile vandalism, occasionally coupled with some perpetrated by adults, was widespread, even becoming more serious after World War II ended. From the beginning Superintendent Hamilton had used it as an argument against the double shift in the schools. He pointed out that 1,750 students were roaming the narrow confines of Vanport both morning and afternoon, forced outside by the smallness of the living units and the lack of parental supervision occasioned by double employment. Truancy was encouraged by the presence of the other shift on the street, cutting attendance in school to 83.3 percent. Creative activities were not possible, either in the home or at school. Hamilton prophesied gang development. Consequently the better parents were already looking for some place else to live. Selden Menefee, in his book *Assignment: U.S.A.*, based on an early tour of the war centers, had noted the rapid delinquency rises there as opposed to the country as a whole, and had appealed for more millions for child-care centers. He realized, too, that most of the new women war workers would want to continue working after the war.[5]

There seemed to be an overwhelming consensus as to the magnitude of the problem, and the vandalism continued throughout the life of the project. In 1944, the board of commissioners discussed the troubles tenants were having with juvenile disturbances and property destruction (the very type of difficulty that administrators like to keep out of the hands of a board). By mid-1945 almost everyone agreed conditions were so bad the problem no longer could just be discussed, but action must be taken.[6]

A review of the situation was assembled in the attempt to obtain FPHA approval for a child welfare department and to secure professional personnel from the Multnomah County Department of Public Welfare. The presentation sketched out how the original plans for Vanport City concentrated on conserving land, therefore there were no private yards or play areas. Full utilization of the nursery schools never occurred, perhaps because there was a small fee. Instead, the children were simply turned loose in the streets, and cases of child neglect multiplied. Visiting teachers were swamped, and the nursery schools had to take in the so-called "lost children." Many walked the one mile to enjoy the undesirable atmosphere of Jantzen Beach Amusement Park. Volunteer groups willing to tackle some of the problems did not exist, and other county agencies considered themselves overloaded with their own problems.[7]

The plea for help further documented Vanport's disorientation. During the preceding year (1 July 1944 to 30 June 1945) 28,919 people had moved in and 28,148 had moved out. These figures accurately reflected movement of children 16 and under—9,496 in and 9,471 out. The result, at the children's level, was "total confusion." The Housing Authority concluded that all the factors merged to form a "lack of normalcy" in the environment—the basic cause of the delinquency.[8] It was correct insofar as the term normalcy applied to past conditions, but unperceived was the beginning of a new normalcy, later to be termed by John Kenneth Galbraith the "affluent society." Money, freely handed out, began to replace attention and personal concern, and lack of supervision was combined with an excess of free time.

In 1943 HAP had requested help from the Multnomah County Welfare Department. In October 1944 the state welfare department approved a budget for Vanport calling for three professional workers, a supervisor, and office help. During November the supervisor arrived to do the planning, took up residence in Vanport, stated the problem was insoluble, and secured a transfer to the county office, all within less than a month. The county administrator was said to be cooperative, but in response to further appeals his reply was that it was impossible to obtain people for the job at the salary offered.[9]

About the only exception to the general unanimity on the seriousness of Vanport's juvenile problems was the opinion of one probation officer. He was quoted in an Oregon *Journal* story saying that Vanport City was the only district in "greater Portland" that showed a de-

cline in juvenile delinquency, a rather curious statement in view of the lack of records. Questions as to the previous incidence and amount of decline remained unanswered. It was also a rare case of the Oregon *Journal* taking a positive view of Vanport. However, the comment was occasioned by the recounting of a highly successful four-day Halloween patrol organized by the Sheriff's Office in cooperation with school and youth groups. Seven to 10 older youngsters were accompanied by a volunteer officer. Thirty-five officers and 300 children were involved. There was not a single report of vandalism to the Sheriff's Office, and no destruction apparently took place. Significantly, one of the Pacific Northwest's heavy rainstorms aided the effort.[10]

As previously noted, the public schools of Vanport tried hard to extend the scope of their activities in order to contend with the massive juvenile problem. They were joined by two volunteer extensions of the Sheriff's Office, namely the Sheriff's Guard and Sheriff's Patrol. The latter two sponsored boxing shows, a band for students beyond elementary school, and a Boy Scout troop.[11] But these efforts, although worthwhile and valuable for many youths, were much like the proverbial finger in the dike. Juvenile vandalism continued on a large scale throughout Vanport's history. Appearing at the time as a huge problem, the attacks nevertheless were confined mainly to property and seem more minor when compared to today's assaults on persons.

Almost as soon as Vanport was fully completed, HAP found it necessary to build a fenced area in which to store what appeared to be abandoned automobiles. Sitting in the parking lots, the cars were being stripped by children and adults. Many were without tires and wheels, while parts from a single car would sometimes be scattered over a fifty foot area. It was common for children to be on the streets at 1:30 A.M. breaking windows, stealing, even occasionallly setting fires. Bathtubs, originally installed in the service buildings for those who could not or did not want to use the showers in the apartments, had to be removed. The Housing Authority of Portland considered a curfew, but the only penalty could have been eviction from the project. This, and the enforcement difficulties inherent in the around-the-clock culture of Vanport caused the idea to be dropped.[12]

Between Christmas and New Years Day 1946, $1,000 worth of window glass was broken. In March 1947, one HAP commissioner stated that destruction in the service buildings was so bad it was impossible to describe. Adding foot policemen was again discussed. The commissioners did not like the Sheriff's Office practice of sometimes shifting the 19 to 22 officers stationed in Vanport to other duties in Multnomah County. At a meeting in June with Sheriff Martin Pratt and Chief Ard Pratt, the brothers reluctantly agreed to discontinue the assignment changes and to add, at HAP expense, seven more officers to patrol the three worst vandalism areas.[13] With the additional patrolmen, the influx of veterans, and the continued growth of Vanport College, the problem lessened during the final year.

There was, of course, crime in Vanport. No really accurate comparison can be made with other parts of the metropolitan area, Multnomah County, or other sections of the nation. Record keeping was inadequate in Multnomah County until after 1946, and conclusive judgments cannot be formed from pre-1946 bits and pieces, such as the Sheriff's station answering more calls in Vanport than in all the rest of Multnomah County. The original Sheriff's Office facilities quickly proved inadequate. Larger and better quarters had to be constructed. However, the jail did include a separate "drunk tank" where the inebriates were segregated from the other prisoners awaiting transport to larger and more secure county facilities.[14]

As might be expected, a series of minor law enforcement problems came out of the city's quick creation. Early traffic enforcement difficulties (because of

Ard M. Pratt was, in effect, the chief of police at Vanport. (OHS neg. 69470)

non-public ownership of the streets) have been previously alluded to. A more serious aspect of the problem was the belief of the Sheriff's Office that only disorderly conduct warrants could be issued for drunken driving (subsequently clarified under state law). Gambling and prostitution remained a "hit or miss" operation, not highly organized. During the early days of 1943, one tobacco concessionaire felt his lease included the right to have pinball games, and when the Sheriff's Office told him it did not, he protested. A raid on the operators of pinball games and punchboards elicited a letter from FPHA to HAP instructing it to tell lessees that if they violated local laws their lease would be subject to cancellation. Throughout the whole of Vanport's history HAP opposed any "tolerance" policy, even refusing the Veterans of Foreign Wars permission to hold a Bingo game.[15] This course of action, so at variance with the situation in Portland itself, resulted from the dictatorial control exercised by the governmental agencies in charge of Vanport. The individual whims of those in power could be more easily forced upon the people, and

Sheriff and Mrs. Martin T. Pratt at a tanker launching ceremony. Sheriff Pratt ran the flood emergency operation. Notice Mrs. Pratt's corsage of ration stamps. (OHS neg. 69454)

the commissioners, who possessed little political experience in this area, wished people to be something they were not.

The anonymity, fluidity, lack of social organization, and population density of Vanport caused concern and apprehension about crime amongst both HAP and the tenants. A large proportion of the residents had come from rural areas of the country where war industry was lacking and crime-conducive conditions did not exist. Perhaps the fear was greater than warranted, although it was related to the potential, and resulted in many statements of alarm. In May 1944, the HAP board of commissioners discussed the rumored carrying of concealed weapons by Vanport citizens. A letter to HAP from FPHA in August expressed concern about the "steady and alarming increase" in the percentage rise in total arrests compared to population. Here, reference should again be made to Chief of Police Ard Pratt's later comment as to the questionable quality of police records. Although FPHA felt the increasing number of blacks may have contributed, the greatest adult delinquency must be ascribed to the white population. There were always a great number of living units not ready for occupancy. The major reason for this was that if the units were renovated before being immediately occupied, in addition to the vandalism hazards, they would be pilfered by other tenants.[16] When World War II ended HAP officials feared the V-J Day celebrations would degenerate into an undefined catastrophe. The Sheriff's Office prepared to meet the threat. With a great deal of relief Manager Q.B. Griffin reported to the commissioners that there had been no disturbance, and he lauded the police for their well organized patrol.[17]

A memorandum sent to Harry Freeman in December 1945 by his chief subordinate K.E. Eckert, illustrated the apprehension and the occasional friction between HAP and the Sheriff's Office (however, all agreed after Vanport's history was over that relations were quite amicable following the first year's misunderstandings). Pratt had assured Eckert that adequate control of gambling and vice was being maintained, but several months had passed and no real effort had been made. Due to recent reports of rape and lawlessness in the newspapers the Sheriff's Office had become a little more active. Eckert received new reports daily of people being afraid to be out after dark (an unusual complaint for that time), and women and children possessed a common fear about being alone in an apartment at night. Because many of the buildings were not visible from the road he had suggested a foot patrol, but Captain Pratt had replied that the precinct already had more staff than was warranted by any equivalent population elsewhere in the county. Finally, returning veterans were talking of taking the law into their own hands, and he had just heard that the Council of Churches was threatening to make a public statement of concern about conditions.[18]

In his criticism of the operations of the Sheriff's Office, Eckert made special reference to one small incident which, in its embellishment, became the type of story that leads to friction and misunderstanding. He felt the Sheriff's Office was trying to discredit and em-barrass HAP employees and used as an example the case of a "dependable" HAP detective who had located some stolen HAP property. The employee went to the Deputy District Attorney for help, and according to Eckert was given the reply that HAP was nothing but "a bunch of damned New-Deal Democrats." He hoped that "all the property would be stolen."[19]

One of the commissioners, in early 1947, was authorized to call on Chief Pratt and threaten calling in federal police to enforce law in the project if conditions did not improve. About all he could get from the Captain was a promise to look into the problem of peddlers (a continuing source of complaints to HAP by Vanport merchants). Then HAP considered taking the money paid to the Multnomah County Sheriff's Office and establishing their own system but wisely thought better of it.[20]

In conclusion it should be stated that there was probably as much crime in Vanport as in other equivalent West Coast population centers. But whether there was a greater or lesser amount of various types remains indeterminable. Certainly, by today's standards, crimes of violence against persons were relatively low, as they were elsewhere in the country.

RACE

Vanport made a lasting contribution in pushing the most populous area in Oregon into the modern world of race relations. Wartime labor shortages induced the Kaiser Company to import sizable numbers of blacks. The effect was catalytic and permanent. Vanport and another smaller project (Guild Lake) provided decent housing along with other satisfactory community conditions.[1] This adequate environment lessened the tensions inherent in the new assimilation problems. Portland was able to make a relatively smooth transition from an era when the black population's existence could be forgotten to an era when the black community became a small but recognized part of the Portland community.

Oregon once had a population of around 3,000 black men and women but the openly hostile attitude of Oregonians had driven this figure to 1,800 at the time of the 1940 census, and almost all of these were in the Portland area where railroad and hotel service jobs were about their only sources of employment. The pre-war and wartime shipyard activity with its attendant labor shortages created concern among some Portlanders over the possibility of the importation of blacks. As early as October 1942, a rumor circulated that the Housing Authority of Portland contemplated building an exclusively black dormitory in Albina. Executive Director Freeman made a vehement denial. Of the approxi-

mately 2,500 workers recruited by Kaiser in New York City late that year, about 300 were black. That wartime activities brought a huge increase in the Portland area's black population was borne out by a 1946 estimate of 15,000, an over 800 percent increase.[2]

During the expansionary period of shipyard activity the black population of Vanport did not reach levels greatly above its percentage of the national population. It was only when yard orders declined that proportions rose drastically as whites left and a much larger proportion of black workers remained. Whether this was due to having no place to go or whether they felt living conditions at Vanport justified staying remains unclear.

Of the first 1,547 project units rented (December 1942 and January 1943), only 41 were occupied by blacks. By October 1943 the black population in Vanport had risen to approximately 1,500, still under 5 percent of the project's population at the time. During 1944 proportionate numbers of blacks rose steadily until they constituted slightly over 17 percent of the total, an estimate based on unit occupancy (5,328 blacks, 25,242 whites). However, it was in 1945 that proportions rose dramatically, and the Vanport concentration overwhelmed that of any other HAP project.[3]

The highest occupancy in the project's history was reached during January and February 1945. After this, shipyard orders began to decline and approximately 500 white families left Vanport each month until September, when the rate accelerated following the end of the war. During this same period the black population increased very slightly until June, rose more rapidly during the summer, and took a sizable drop with the war's end, although not nearly as large as the white reduction. In January 1945 black families constituted 18 percent of the total number of families. By October the proportion had risen to 35 percent. As early as March 1945 there were over three-and-a-half times as many black families in Vanport as there were in all other HAP projects combined.[4] From 1946 on, total population levels did not change materially, and racial ratios underwent no further significant change.

Vanport brought to the greater Portland area an awareness of race and the possibility of racial problems, in itself an important contribution. In October 1943, the Portland City Club asked City Manager J.L. Franzen about the "Negro living problem." By mid-1944 the influx was causing general concern. Superintendent of Schools James T. Hamilton contacted the chairman of the HAP Board of Commissioners to express his apprehension. Harry Freeman reported that the Kaiser Company planned on bringing in 5,000 more new workers, 28 percent of whom would be "colored," and he suggested that a discussion should be held with the management division and the Vanport Manager in order to formulate a definite policy. Chairman Gartrell expressed what had largely remained unsaid, that Vanport City was becoming "tagged" as a "Negro Project," and that this stereotyping ought to be stopped. The Executive Committee of the Portland Chamber of Commerce, in a June 28 letter to Harry Freeman, listed the "Negro problem" as one of the factors in the unsatisfactory housing conditions at Vanport, which in turn led to a heavy manpower turnover.[5]

By the end of 1944 the Portland *Oregonian* had accepted the idea that most of the black men and women who migrated to the region during the war would stay, and recommended that the community accept the new residents. To substantiate its position, it used author Carey McWilliams' prediction that 85 percent of the black workers who moved to the West Coast during this period would remain, and the paper further quoted the National Association of Real Estate Boards to the effect that Negroes maintain property in about the same condition as whites in the same income categories. The trouble was that most of the property they could get was old and in poor condition.[6]

Thus the existence of a problem came to be recognized and the necessity of dealing with it accepted, although Harry Freeman sometimes felt that excessive talk helped create a larger problem than actually existed. In June 1945 HAP received a written request from the Vanport Inter-Racial Council and a verbal one from the Portland Urban League. Both wished hearings on, as the Urban League put it, "economic and social situations," at Vanport. Two separate sessions were held. A 7 September HAP letter to FPHA dealing with the Vanport Recreation Association conflict then taking place also made reference to the possibility of larger race relations difficulties.[7]

Aside from the arguments over housing segregation (considered later), there was little, if any, official racial discrimination or, for that matter, any serious racial incidents. The vast number of leases for business operations of all types, including the hospital, contained the federally required provision that no qualified employee or applicant shall be discriminated against because of race, creed, color, national origin, or political affiliation, and there never were any serious charges of violations. By the time black occupancy reached 12 percent (August 1944) two black policemen were employed by the Sheriff's Office and two more were on the HAP investigative staff. Kilbourn and Lantis in their early study of tenant dissatisfactions stated, almost casually, that there was a non-discrimination policy in public places, recreation buildings, and schools. Chief of Police Ard Pratt felt the department had no unusual problems, and that blacks and whites got along quite well. He felt that whatever incidents did occur were between individuals and not groups, and the situation was much better than at other large projects such as the one in Vallejo, California.[8]

Vanport gave the Portland area a framework within which it could find its own solutions to racial tensions during a time period when the problem was not so severe as to polarize community attitudes. It helped Portland create a pattern of pragmatically seeking solutions, a method which would operate more effectively than the process taking place in other major West Coast cities.

This experimentation and "feeling the way" was quickly illustrated in an early Vanport incident. Blacks settled into what became known as the Negro section of Vanport. Whether this was by HAP design became hotly debated. This area contained Recreation Center Number 5. Some of the social workers employed by HAP, particularly those at the recreation centers, were looking for opportunities to promote inter-racial mixing, hoping that this would lead to better racial understanding. A black committee approached Manager J.L. Franzen with a proposal that they sponsor a War Bond drive for one week, a part of which would be the holding of a dance each night at the Recreation Center (during the war period blacks usually were more active than whites in community affairs). Attendance by a racially mixed crowd was expected.[9]

The committee sponsoring the dance did not particularly approve of mixed dancing, but the recreation director at the center formulated plans to encourage it.

The deputy sheriff assigned to the dance reported that it started when a Negro entered and began dancing with his Jewish wife. Black men then asked the white girls, and it was mostly teen-agers who responded. The director (a Miss Saulsman) danced with several "colored" men. During these developments the white couples tended to leave. When some of those present asked the deputy what he was going to do, he replied, nothing until he got instructions, and he then predicted a great number of complaints. His observations were not exactly impartial, as he reported "several known Communists" encouraging white girls to dance with the "colored."[10]

Investigative officers, called to the dance, found a crowd of white men on the outside making remarks. When the officers entered they observed six white girls dancing with black men and discovered that it had been going on all evening. Upon interviewing Miss Saulsman she gave it her unqualified approval and stated the director of all project recreational activities had specifically instructed them to encourage the mixed dancing. Subsequently the same evening blacks came to Recreation Center Number 2's swing shift dance and danced with whites. The director there requested the officers to stop the practice, but they said they could not unless there was a disturbance. However, the dance was stopped a half hour early at 4:30 A.M. Upon returning to the station the officers interrogated three white girls (sixteen years and under) who were wandering around after the dance with seven "colored" men. The girls had attended both dances, and one stated that Miss Saulsman had asked her to dance with the Negroes. A warning was issued to the girls that such action might lead to a race riot because of the large number of Southerners in the project.[11]

These developments led to a discussion of the issue at the next board of commissioners' meeting. Chief Pratt reported the situation intolerable from a police standpoint and wondered why, since there was no public demand for the mixed dances, they were not stopped—especially their promotion by the recreation supervisors. Harry Freeman referred to a black minister's letter, recently sent to Washington, D.C., alleging discrimination and segregation in Vanport. Chairman Gartrell mused about the effect of the Presidential order on non-discrimination in housing projects and wondered about the establishment of a separate recreation hall for Negroes.[12] Fortunately this plan was dropped, and facilities remained open to all, even though used primarily by blacks or whites.

Vanport's lack of adult recreation outlets affected blacks as well as whites, and in the summer of 1946, HAP courageously opened itself to criticism by entertaining a proposal for a lunch, card, and billiard room in Nursery Number 1, to be run by a black operator in a black area of Vanport. Although it was designed to meet

Original newspaper caption: "No color line here—Daily vacation Bible school in Vanport City at Recreation Center No. 5 ministers to all who attend, regardless of race." (OHS neg. 78869)

the needs of black residents, white residents were not excluded. The Housing Authority also hoped the recommended facility would reduce gambling in private apartments. The proposal was finally approved in October and the "Oasis" was run for 18 months by operator Ken Smith. At that time he wished to sell the lease, but there was some pressure to allow Vanport College to use the building. The Housing Authority did, however, transfer the lease to another operator.[13]

The discrimination that did exist (aside from the question of housing) was not due to HAP policy but to the actions of single individuals. There was a complete lack of any organized promotion of discriminatory treatment. As Ken Smith put it, he had always enjoyed good relations with the HAP Commissioners (who also felt he had done a good job), but certain employees of HAP gave him "a bad time." It was the old story of the difficulty of carrying policy down through the ranks. Of course there were some personal incidents among residents, but as Chief Pratt indicated the "situation was not bad."[14]

Whether blacks contributed a more than proportionate share of criminal activity remains indeterminable. Portland Police Chief Harry Niles charged Negroes with committing the bulk of knife and gun incidents in the Portland area but without records to back up the claim. There was general agreement that, starting with the war, and then accelerating during the postwar period, a sharp rise occurred in both white and black major crime. Portland received its share of both blacks and whites with criminal records, and many used the shipyards as a legitimate front. There, an individual could be guilty of chronic absenteeism and not be fired. Vanport was the only place with crime statistics, and as Chief Pratt mentioned, their compiling left much to be desired. One might argue, for instance, as the Portland *Oregonian* did, that black and white crime ratios in Vanport were the same. From 1 July 1943 to 30 June 1944 there were 1,176 white arrests to 244 black, approximately five to one, nearly the same ratio as the populaton. Conversely, in April, May, and June of 1944 the Sheriff's Office reported that blacks made up 30 percent of arrests, while HAP estimates, based on apartments occupied, gave them 18 percent of Vanport's population.[15] Thus a conclusive statement cannot be made.

As previously mentioned, the black population tended, during the wartime years, to participate more actively than whites in HAP attempts to get Vanporters involved in community activities. This even extended into the realm of religion, and blacks formed the largest congregation in the United Church Ministry at Vanport. Average Sunday attendance at services held in their section of Vanport was 300, deemed unusual enough for the Oregon *Journal* to carry a picture of the congregation.[16]

With the end of the war, blacks quickly faced a problem that would trouble them far into the future. In July 1945, 7,000 non-whites were employed in the area's shipyards. By November the number was down to 1,500 and still dropping. There were few new job opportunities for those laid off. Only personal service jobs were available. Consequently, Vanport delinquent accounts soon showed blacks to have a rate more than twice that of whites.[17] Thus, while Vanport provided the housing to enable the country to move part of its black labor pool into an area where it was badly needed, it was not able, as economic conditions became more normal, to counter long-term social trends.

At Vanport, HAP was faced with a problem new to the region, how to house large numbers of blacks and whites in close proximity. Vanport's major racial controversy arose in connection with this, and it spanned the life of the project. By today's standards, however, it was muted and dealt only with whether the segregation that admittedly existed was the result of black desires or HAP design. It had nothing to do with the quality of the housing, which remained the same for blacks and whites.

91

As pointed out earlier, previous to the war, blacks represented a rather small proportion of Portland's population. Most Portlanders felt they were concentrated on the east side of the Willamette River in the Albina District. This was not true. The approximately 2,000 blacks in Portland in 1940 were distributed throughout 53 of the 60 census tracts. There were 653 in the largest, and 350 in the second largest, but this still left approximately 1,000 distributed throughout almost all areas. Thus, despite any public opinion to the contrary, blacks were not segregated in any one or two areas, and an early report examining recreational facilities for blacks in Vanport (made without HAP knowledge) matter-of-factly stated that the Portland area had never had any racial difficulties during the preceding years.[18] Of course it had never had a sizable black population either.

The majority of blacks, as they arrived in increasing numbers, were quietly settled in Vanport. It soon became apparent that they were concentrated in three areas, mainly in the vicinity of Cottonwood Street. How it had happened, and whether it should be allowed to continue were questions that were argued for almost the entire life of the project. Outside groups, both black and white, added their voices to those of Vanport residents.

De facto segregation clearly existed, and its presence was not seriously argued by anyone. Incidental mention of the "colored section" was sometimes made in police officers' reports. Kilbourn and Lantis made reference to the three areas in their early study. However, it was not patently clear that HAP was responsible. An early report on recreational facilities for blacks made a complimentary remark on the location of Negro families in several sections of Vanport. As late as March 1944, a complaint letter to HAP listed, among other things, the objection that "There is also only a very vague attempt to segregate negroes from white people here." Things would be improved if they were ". . . Keep [sic] off to their selves better."[19]

From the beginning HAP Executive Director Harry Freeman and the board of commissioners were aware of the potential racial problem, and they had to plot a course in uncharted waters. They decided to house blacks only at Vanport and one other project. Because of the relative size of the two projects and the number of people involved, this meant Vanport must take the bulk of them. In July 1943 the decision was made not to allow 42 black families having a member employed at Commercial Iron Works to move into housing units being constructed for this industry. By this time units at Vanport being held for black workers were filled, and it was with relief that HAP greeted the opening of additional housing in adjacent Vancouver, Washington, and the Vancouver Housing Authority's willingness to take blacks from Vanport if they were employed in the Vancouver yards. In August HAP commissioners held two lengthy discussions on racial problems. The board minutes merely carried a mention of their being held, without including any information.[20]

By October requests for information and protests on racial policy made it necessary for HAP to take an open position, even though Harry Freeman believed the less discussion about it the better, a position he took in response to Mayor Earl Riley's request for information to be included in an American Municipal Association booklet. Freeman stated, for the record, "in all honesty" there was no racial problem in any of the projects, including Vanport City, and the 1,500 Negroes in Vanport (still considerably less than 10 percent) wanted harmony as much as did the whites.[21]

One of Vanport's ministers, the Reverend James Clow, sent a letter directly to the national office of FPHA charging housing segregation and discrimination. When the letter made its way back to the Seattle Regional Office, Freeman had to reply. His explanation was that when first assigned to Vanport living units they were given the buildings available at the time. It so happened that these were in three general areas. Subsequently

92

Reverend James Clow, pastor of the Mt. Olivet Baptist Church and past president of the Portland branch of the NAACP, served as a spokesman for the black community of Vanport. (OHS neg. CN 001398)

all the Negro families at Vanport, whereupon he was asked by Freeman if they were satisfied and happy. He replied, "happy and content." Freeman then argued that most of the allegations came from those not connected with Vanport.[22]

Whether this was the way Vanport's segregation originated and was maintained is not clear from the records. Harry Freeman and HAP consistently held to this position. It does appear that HAP kept separate waiting lists and files. Board minutes for 18 May 1944 made reference to 267 "colored" families on the waiting list for Vanport. At this time there were vacancies in the project. The Housing Authority was trying to arrive at what, in its opinion, was the most desirable solution for a problem and to keep that solution within the framework of federal rules. The federal position seemed clearly against any segregation, yet a secret memo in May 1944 to City Manager J.L. Franzen from the Management Division of HAP on its Negro housing policy declared policy could be based on local cultural patterns, and although blacks lived in most sections of Portland, still there was limited segregation. Thus, HAP could locate blacks in a very few projects, which it did, and the only one left that could take any more was Vanport.[23] One thing was certain, HAP did not feel that one of its duties was to initiate social change.

Whether HAP liked it or not, Vanport soon became a sizable sociological experiment. By mid-1944, the black population passed the 10 percent mark. Widespread concern was expressed by almost all Vanport groups about the racial housing policy, and while not so openly acknowledged by HAP, its concern continued. The Sheriff's Office and HAP's Project Services division were both worried about the possible increase in incidents of physical violence, perhaps even a race riot, while the Recreation Department felt apprehension about whites not patronizing four of the community buildings, thus providing these facilities with an exclusively black clientele. Vanport's Public Schools worried

they were given a choice, and they freely chose these sections. In the midst of the controversy the National Housing Association called a meeting to explore the racial situation. Reverend Clow stated that he had visited over racial balance in the school centers. The Public Health Department wanted information as to whether HAP accepted the acknowledged nationwide differential between health standards for Negroes and whites. Racial incidents had a disturbing effect on members of the Vanport Businessmen's Association. The United Church Ministry, which all agreed exercised a stabilizing influence, argued it needed to know for planning purposes if four areas were going to become black concentrations. If so, it felt this would interfere drastically with their operations. All were concerned with the increasing percentage of black occupancy.[24]

In spite of HAP's reluctance to indicate just exactly what it was doing in housing the increasing number of black in-migrants (28 percent by April 1944), white residents of Vanport soon had the situation assessed quite accurately. Rumors circulated that HAP planned to house all Negroes at Vanport City. Large numbers of white tenants then began moving out. Project Services believed morale was disintegrating, a rather unusual observation as there was little favorable comment on morale since the first few months of the project's operation. Apparently feeling some pressure to adhere more closely to the federal government's anti-segregation policy statement, HAP quietly decided on moving incoming blacks into yet another area. Word of this spread, and HAP received a handwritten protest on personal letter paper, bearing 63 scrawled signatures and addresses of people in the proposed section. They advised HAP that there were entire buildings vacant in the black district along Cottonwood Street and recommended keeping them there. The Housing Authority still would make no definitive statement, and the 15 June 1944 minutes carried a vague reference to an "off the record" discussion where "apparently present policies met the approval of those present."[25]

Thus, it was patently clear by mid-1944, despite official silence, that HAP was moving all blacks request- ing housing into Vanport City, and was moving them only into certain specific sections. Because of the wartime housing shortage the practical effect of this action was the placing of all black in-migrants to the Portland area in these particular parts of Vanport. Acknowledgement of the situation sometimes slipped inadvertently into HAP reports. A cleaning and repairing report in September 1944 made reference to the last occupancy listing, which showed that out of 597 applications for housing 283 were "colored." The report then stated it would be necessary to move white families out of the "designated colored areas" in order to accommodate the black families.[26]

An unpublicized, official admission of what it was doing was finally forced out of HAP in March 1945. A protest letter written by a black woman to Eleanor Roosevelt triggered the acknowledgement. The woman complained that she could not get an apartment the size she wanted while whites were able to, and appealed to Mrs. Roosevelt to help her. When the letter returned through channels, HAP answered. It admitted the charge might be true because of its policy of alternating blocks of apartments for blacks and whites for "integration purposes." The Housing Authority thought the policy had worked well, and that both groups were satisfied. However, it entailed the keeping of separate waiting lists, and because of this the situation stated by the complainant might have occurred. The Authority promised to make available the unit she was requesting as soon as possible.[27] It still was not ready for any public disclosures, as approximately a week later, in response to a letter of inquiry from the City Club of Portland, it gave the usual vague reply, "As you know there can be no racial discrimination in housing any war worker in Federally-owned [sic] dwellings."[28]

Throughout this time, although certainly aware of HAP's policy, FPHA pursued a "hands off" attitude. In fact, relations were extremely cordial during the whole

94

period of F.M. Crutsinger's regional directorship. A new element was injected in mid-1945 when Crutsinger resigned to become director of the Foreign Shelter Division. He was replaced in Seattle by Jesse Epstein, the executive director of the Seattle Housing Authority. Immediately HAP set out to clear its policies with the new leadership. Chairman Moores met with Epstein and, in effect, received the green light for HAP to continue on its present course. Moores reported that Epstein considered the housing of minorities to be a local problem and up to the local Authority, that various methods were adaptable for various cities, and what had been done in Seattle was not necessarily applicable elsewhere. So segregation by "blocks" continued, and although the Urban League and American Veterans' Committee proposed a "non-segregation" policy at a meeting with HAP officials in March 1946, little came of the effort.[29]

Rather ironically, the first real confrontation over HAP housing policy occurred when the Authority planned to accede to newly developing Vanport College's request for additional buildings in a black section. As rumors of the pending action spread, a Portland black newspaper, the *Northwest Clarion* took up the battle. It declared HAP was moving blacks to a much less desirable area, that this had happened twice before, and that HAP had finally been forced to admit the purpose was to clear the area for white veterans. This had come into the open only when a black veterans' group, meeting with Vanport City Manager Harry Jaeger, had been shown the letter from Oregon State System of Higher Education (OSSHE) requesting they vacate the buildings. A protest letter had been dispatched to Regional Director Epstein, along with the admonition that, if the reply was not satisfactory, it would be necessary to go to Washington, D.C. Finally the newspaper concluded with this advice to black residents, "DON'T BUDGE—DON'T MOVE." In this manner ". . . you will smoke out THE STRANGER IN THE WOODPILE."[30]

Edwin C. Berry was executive secretary of the Portland Urban League and was active in racial issues at Vanport. This 1955 photo shows him being presented with the American Veteran's Committee Freedom Award. (OHS neg. 69460)

At the board of commissioners' meeting on 17 October 1946, Edwin C. Berry presented the views of the Urban League of Portland, which represented the interests of Vanport's black residents. Chairman Herbert J. Dahlke vehemently denied HAP had ever discriminated and upbraided Ellis Ash (area supervisor for FPHA, who was present) for implying that they had. His parting shot was that if FPHA ever wanted those particular units for transfer to another location it was going to have to come to Portland and handle the job. As previously noted OSSHE withdrew its request, and HAP approval of it was rescinded. Blacks were allowed to remain in the segregated area, and from that time on, when Vanport College requested additional buildings for office space or other uses, the request was carefully cleared through the Urban League, and housing arrangements were made that were satisfactory to the black tenants.[31]

Vanport's segregated housing pattern continued throughout 1947 and apparently even began to worsen. The flow of black in-migrants ceased as job opportunities disappeared in the postwar period. Much of Vanport's black population stayed, as few of them had any place else to go. Many of the remaining whites, living either in the segregated sections or on their periphery moved out of Vanport or to other sections of it where there now was plenty of available housing. A rather bizarre touch to the whole situation was provided when a black Portlander submitted a proposal to HAP to buy an unspecified number of Vanport apartment buildings for permanent residences for "colored people." Because of the legal problems, and perhaps for other reasons, HAP did not consider the offer. Incoming whites would not accept units in or on the edge of black areas, so black concentrations became even more noticeable. When blacks from Guild Lake (a smaller project and the only other one with a concentration of black residents) questioned why was there segregation in Vanport when the policy was non-segregation, Freeman replied that whites would not accept units in those areas and other Portland area Negroes applied for and were willing to take those apartments, which were undoubtedly better than they could secure elsewhere.[32]

It was a portent of a trend that would accelerate in American cities in the coming years. As the 1968 Interim Report of the Special Advisory Commission on Civil Disorders pointed out, 20 percent of the residents in the average neighborhood in the United States moved every year, and they would not move into "changing" areas, thus causing these areas to eventually become almost totally black.[33]

Maintaining its Vanport policy until 1948, HAP only abandoned it under a pressure onslaught from the Portland Housing and Planning Association. A resolution of the Association received full publicity in the *Oregonian* prior to its presentation to HAP. It charged HAP had publicly avowed non-discrimination and non-segregation while in fact practicing it. What HAP had done was in fact much worse than anything in Seattle, San Francisco, or Los Angeles, and the resolution demanded HAP state publicly that equal treatment would be given, which meant all housing should be on a first-come, first-served basis.[34]

Monsignor Thomas J. Tobin, president of the Portland Housing and Planning Association, presented the resolution at the 8 January board of commissioners' meeting. Additionally he read from a letter by the FPHA's regional race adviser to the effect that "complete segregation" existed in the Portland facilities. The Housing Authority made its usual response, a denial of intent to segregate, that the choices were made by Negroes themselves, and put off the resolution for further study. It then quietly decided to throw in the towel. At a meeting with representatives of the League of Women Voters on 5 February, HAP assured them that it intended to practice no discrimination or segregation by race. The next day Chairman Herbert J. Dahlke maintained at a meeting at Portland City Hall that the issue had arisen because whites would not move into "colored" areas. And perhaps he was partially right, although no one will ever know what might have happened if, from the beginning, black families had been assigned to housing in Vanport on a "hit or miss" basis, and thus spread irregularly throughout the whole city. At any rate an order was quietly issued to Harry Jaeger to accept applications on a first-come, first-served basis. Edwin Berry felt it made little impact on the overall Portland situation because it applied to Vanport only, and at Vanport 90 percent of the remaining units

96

were occupied, and what vacancies did exist were largely in the black area.[35] Because of the short remaining period of Vanport's life, the new policy had impact only as a continuation of the process of peaceful change.

Vanport City, despite its short life, provided the housing and community services which allowed the importation of sizable numbers of blacks into the Portland area. There they were incorporated into the life of the region with a minor amount of friction. This may have been because they were willing at the time to accept "half a loaf," or it may have been that HAP's middle of the road policy, combined with pushes and shoves from both extremes, was best for that time and place. Whatever the reason, serious troubles were avoided, and Portlanders finally accepted and acknowledged the existence of a black community as a permanent part of the area's life. When the flood disaster struck, the black citizens of Vanport especially had no place to go and gargantuan efforts were made by Portlanders to provide for them, both temporarily and permanently.

THE IMAGE

Vanport captured the public's imagination. People reacted to its imagery with intensity, sometimes favorably, sometimes unfavorably. It's indefinable qualities triggered strong feelings and memories. Young children who had no direct contact with Vanport recall it from emotional comments made by their parents. During its short life very few calm, dispassionate judgments of the city were ever made. In the beginning there was an overwhelming outpouring of favorable publicity. Certain aspects of the project were almost completely overlooked, such as its compactness, around-the-clock life, density of population, fire danger, lack of individual property ownership, and planned temporary wartime life: characteristics that would create problems and attitudes reversing the overly complimentary early image. The picture then turned to one of extreme disfavor, while the truth lay hidden somewhere in between.

Because Vanport City was different and was not just another wartime federal housing project, both the national and local informational media combined at the start to create a super aura around Vanport. Construction and planning was done by the Kaiser Company, not the Federal Public Housing Administration, and thus Henry J. Kaiser's giant image as the master shipbuilder was transferred to the city. The project had the first public library designed exclusively for a housing develop-ment and the largest public school system—it was even second in size in the state of Oregon. *Business Week* termed it "the nation's newest, most unusual city," while *Arts and Architecture* described it as a "super project." Portland's *Daily Journal of Commerce* called it the "Northwest's unique sociological experiment" and stated there is "nothing like it anywhere in the country." [1]

An article in *Western City Magazine*, written by Harry Freeman, described the wartime community as not only providing shelter "but many of the conditions of normal, happy living as well." One of Portland's newspapers ran a large picture of the architect's attractive sketch of the basic apartment building. In a lengthy story in the Oregon *Journal* in June 1943 the landscape architects commissioned for the project stated, "Vanport City should be a garden spot by another spring." The *Bo's'n's Whistle*, a wartime magazine of the three Kaiser shipyards in the area, carried an extremely laudatory account. A Vanport family appeared in the *Oregonian* in the "Home of the Week" along with five pictures. Upon completion of the project, the *Oregonian* used approximately a half-page for a fine aerial photograph of the city and titled it, "Vanport, Masterpiece of Urban Planning, Thrives as City of Homes." In the beginning there was not even much native antipathy towards the mass influx of newcomers. Although usu-

An aerial view of the Vanport housing project. (OHS neg. 68762)

ally somewhat addicted to sensationalism, the Oregon *Journal*'s rational assessment was that perhaps a few Oregonians did resent them, but the great majority did not. The newcomers were doing an important job in a war that had vast public support.[2]

The prestigious journal, *Architectural Forum*, featured Vanport City in its August 1943 issue. On the title page was this description, "The country's largest war housing project is also the most complete . . . an emergency design for an emergency community which fulfills its function with remarkable efficiency." Vanport was contrasted with the "monumental failure" and "never built town" at Willow Run, where something like it might have done for bombers what housing around Portland did for ships.[3]

Portland General Electric Company (PGE), the project's electrical supplier, commissioned four different artists to paint an oil or water color of "Life in Vanport." These slightly impressionistic paintings were then reproduced, and on the back of each was a very optimistic written interpretation of some of the features of Vanport life, such as its schools, recreation, religion, and the status of democracy there. Two of the titles indicated the feeling portrayed by the paintings. They were "Day Nursery in the Tree Shaded Park" and "Sandlot Baseball in the Sunshine."[4]

A full page advertisement in Portland's two major newspapers announced the paintings. The page also contained two coupons, one of which would provide each Vanport family with a free set of the paintings, and the other (for a $3.00 charge) would deliver a set to any address in the United States. The Housing Authority of Portland distributed many additional copies to other geographic areas of the country. The whole gambit turned out to be a tremendous publicity and public relations success, even drawing a letter of commendation from the National Housing Commissioner in Washington, D.C.[5]

Vanport's early national exposure as an innovative attack on war housing problems brought a large number of inquiries to HAP. After Harry Freeman's article in *Western City Magazine* the Commissioner of the American Public Health Association wanted information on health problems. Presumably because Vanport was serving as the chief source of housing for imported blacks, the Pittsburgh *Courier*, which claimed to be the world's largest Negro weekly, wanted data and pictures. However, most requests for information came from various groups concerned with some phase of city planning.[6] Vanport seemed an ideal experimental situation, because here was a sizable city where planners could do what they wanted, and the residents could not stop them.

During this early period (1943) very little to negate this favorable image was published anywhere. The Housing Authority itself had questioned the wisdom of the project while the Kaiser Company was in control of the planning and building, but when HAP became associated with the national publicity, it basked in the limelight and did all it could to stifle exposure of any of Vanport's inherent weaknesses. Thus the proposed *Saturday Evening Post* article by the Cases was successfully suppressed, and an article appearing in the national Catholic monthly magazine *Extension*, which commented unfavorably on the distance Vanport Catholics must go to attend church, drew a critical letter from Harry Freeman. The magazine felt, and correctly, that the letter insinuated the author's complaint demonstrated a lack of patriotism. It sent a hot reply to Freeman and copies of Freeman's letter and the reply to the Archbishop in Portland. Another of the early exceptions to the general rule was the Oregon *Journal*'s attempt to take advantage of Vanport's news value. It concocted a bold, main, front page headline, "VANPORT VICE CHARGED," out of a rather routine Multnomah County Sheriff's Office investigation in which a few houses were found being used for "immoral conduct," with some racial involvement.[7] But these few dissonances hardly dented the overall image.

During 1944, from the sources of public information, it was possible to get the most accurate picture of Vanport City. It was a neutral period where reports did achieve a reasonable balance. There were accurate, complimentary stories such as the declaration by FPHA's fire and safety engineer that Vanport had the best fire protection of any public housing region in the United States. These alternated with articles about the number of tenants leaving and the growing vacancies, but with admonitions against the prevalent loose talk about Vanport being "half empty." Letters to the editor in regard to the noise, the unruly children, and the cramping of individuality by project rules began to appear. Fulton Lewis Jr., the nationally famous radio news commentator, came to Portland for a special broadcast in which he lauded HAP and blamed what he termed the excessive cost of Vanport City on federal intervention.[8]

Gradually the view of Vanport was shifting towards the time soon to come when living in Vanport marked a resident as inferior, of a lower class of society. Additional factors besides the built-in problems were coming to the fore. Exaggerated stories of the living habits of the migrants who had come from poorer sections of the country, especially the South, had had time to circulate widely. Vanport could be focused on as something that represented the outlander. As the prospect of wartime victory lessened the need of Vanporters' contributions and as wartime tensions and frustrations became burdensome, Vanport offered a convenient outlet on which to vent some of these frustrations. The Oregon *Journal* could not resist the temptation of building circulation by magnifying Vanport incidents.

The commissioners were concerned about the image reversal. In August 1944, one commented on the growing amount of unfavorable publicity and the need for some that would be more beneficial. Their legal counselor suggested hiring a feature writer to prepare articles on happier tenants, using funds that had been placed in the budget for publicity purposes. In February 1945 the Commissioners decided to produce a documentary film on Vanport City, but FPHA said money could not be used for that.[9] It was one of those decisions, that in retrospect, should not have been made, as there is very little in the way of a motion picture record of this colorful part of Oregon's and the nations' history.[10] In the end all that was done was the publication of *From Roses to Rivets* (some copies were hard-bound, some paper), which was mainly a collection of statistical and pictorial information on HAP operations. By the time it was published in 1946, the picture of Vanport it portrayed, that of a "Miracle City" and "one of the marvels of the war effort," no longer remained in the public mind, and it had neither much circulation nor effect.[11]

During 1945, written and official comment became almost universally unfavorable. In a magazine article that appeared in March, Superintendent Hamilton of the Vanport Public Schools repeated one of the original comments about Vanport, "It has everything but a future," then proceeded to point out its deficiencies. In July, Chairman Moores reported National Housing Authority Commissioner Philip Klutznick's statement that Vanport City was the most difficult housing problem in the country. The commissioners were refusing to make repairs and necessary additional installations (fire alarms, athletic field restrooms), even against FPHA wishes, because they believed the project should and would be phased out soon. When the war ended the commissioners unanimously agreed Vanport City should be first on the demolition list. By December, some veterans were returning, and when Harry Freeman was asked if HAP would have difficulty in providing housing for these veterans he replied, only when relatives and friends had told them stories about Vanport and advised them not to go there. According to Freeman, Portland was one of five major cities in the United States with a housing surplus, but the trouble was that it was in Vanport.[12]

The pendulum had swung from one extreme point almost to the other. Just as the original picture was not correct, neither was the subsequent one. Vanport residents did not feel this way about their town. A survey taken during this period indirectly demonstrated general satisfaction. The survey's title and basic informational objective was "How Long Do You Plan To Live In This Project?" One thousand two hundred and twenty tenants responded to the 15 choices. The choices indicating dissatisfaction drew only 81 checks (wish to move if possible—four, until better housing available—64, no longer than necessary—13). Of the choices indicating satisfaction or at least a lack of disaffection, the three greatest were: as long as Vanport exists—450, as long as employed—296, and undecided—156. There were few complaint letters from tenants considering the size of the project and the problems involved. There were also letters expressing appreciation for the children's recreation programs, housing, and life in Vanport.[13]

During the first half of 1946, Vanport's image hit bottom, and bottom was a long ways down. As many more whites than blacks moved out with the ending of the war, it became tagged as a black project (which it never was). The "Vanport Fire Bug" set 10 fires during December 1945 and January 1946. Both public buildings and private apartments were involved. In addition to the fear and apprehension, there was over $200,000 damage. A 17 year-old youth was arrested in mid-January, but a second arsonist appeared. Fortunately, the fires finally stopped.[14] The area newspapers really began to concentrate on Vanport. It provided an opportunity to take up some of the slack in spectacular news that followed the

war's end. In February, one of the HAP commissioners rather plaintively wondered why the "shootings, scrapes and the like" could not be relegated to "City Briefs" instead of the first pages.[15]

Added to the racial and criminal picture of Vanport was the welfare stigma. In May the Multnomah County Welfare Commission requested HAP help on the great surge of cases in Vanport, reasoning that the residents had been brought by the shipyards and assigned to housing by HAP. Harry Freeman's response was to check with FPHA, which eventually secured Congressional authorization to expand the veteran's adjusted rent program, and this was done in order to help the Welfare Commission.[16]

This poor image permeated the local scene and began to spread nationally. Superintendent of Schools James T. Hamilton had written to Senator Wayne Morse as early as January 1946 that he was "thoroughly of the opinion" that neither the Vanport schools nor Vanport City should be continued any longer than housing conditions made absolutely necessary. Vanport became the only HAP project with units available for immediate occupancy. All hospitals in Portland were operating at capacity except at Vanport where, in spite of good doctors and excellent care, patients were scarce, except for charity ones. Nine professional baseball players from the Portland Beavers refused housing at Vanport until being shown through the project, then they expressed satisfaction with it. Harry Freeman noted that veterans applying for housing were "almost unanimously" opposed to Vanport, and even Freeman reinforced the image, when he answered, "Vanport will serve until something better comes along."[17]

At this low point Vanport became an outlet for the Portland area's individual and community frustrations. There was just enough truth to sustain the image. Vanport always had HAP's greatest cashier's shortages. There was the vandalism, the newspaper distortions, and the greater than average concentrations of blacks and welfare cases. Vanport citizens felt the impact of community disdain, so much so in fact, that at times some almost developed a persecution complex, resulting in such beliefs as that there was some sort of conspiracy among suppliers to provide Vanport stores with worse food than other Portland outlets.

In mid-1946 a new image began to take hold. The "Veteran's Village" had been established. The Oregon State Board of Higher Education opened Vanport Extension Center. Portland newspapers, in their usual overplay, shifted to paeans of praise for the new developments. There was an increasing number of requests for additional commercial space. A new community spirit arose, exhibiting itself in controversies over the public schools and HAP policy. It even seemed that Vanport City might have a new future. Instead of avoiding Vanport housing, people began to seek it. Lewis and Clark College of Portland contacted FPHA in Seattle about eligibility for housing for staff members, since they were now engaged in the teaching of veterans.[18]

While the changing image was closer to the truth than either the overwhelmingly favorable one at the start or the opposite extreme of early 1946, there was still a more accurate middle ground. Welfare cases in the project continued to rise, with attendant problems. These tenants did considerable damage to some of the apartment units. The Housing Authority, which had always tried to give the taxpayers their money's worth, insisted the Multnomah County Welfare Commission pay for the damage, or at least put up security deposits as the other residents were forced to do. The commission refused and would not even guarantee the rent payments on cases they placed in Vanport. The Housing Authority was frustrated, but felt it had to put up with the situation, and, understandably, other non-welfare tenants did not appreciate this development. By late 1947, 41 percent of all Vanporters were on adjusted rents (welfare,

servicemen, non-welfare low income). In spite of the efforts of many residents during the last two years of the project's life to improve their living quarters and exterior surroundings, an air of general dilapidation prevailed. There were many broken windows. One HAP commissioner reported seeing one apartment building with only one unit occupied, and every other window in the structure broken.[19]

This last, more favorable image of a positive community, acting and participating in the region's life, had emerged and taken hold locally by the time of the flood disaster, but it had not had time to fully penetrate into the consciousness of the national news media. Additionally, HAP commissioners in Portland, along with housing officials in some other communities, were being simplistically charged as obstructionists to new conceptions of public housing. When Vanport, by its sudden disappearance, became a world-wide news spectacular, the nation's press reincarnated the very worst image and passed it on to posterity. Not atypical was *Newsweek*'s reference to the "jerrymade prefabricated homes," and the *New Republic* declared that a quotation from a four-year-old girl rescued from a tree "nicely expressed the feelings of the whole community. 'Daddy, I'm glad Vanport washed away. I don't want to live there any more.'"[20]

Thus the Vanport drama took on some of the characteristics of classic tragedy. Through its birth and early life great achievements seemed to lie ahead. Overlooked were those many factors that by 1946 stigmatized it as something the region would be better off without. It struggled valiantly to recapture its early destiny and appeared, at least locally, to be succeeding. But before it could fix this image in history it died, and the nation's press laid it to rest as an abject failure. Perhaps the later judgment of history will help to recreate a truer picture.

OBLIVION

Although Vanport City sat in the midst of the flood plain of the Columbia River, there had never been any real concern for its safety. In 1943 The *Bo's'n's Whistle*, a wartime magazine of the three Kaiser shipyards in the area, had carried an extremely laudatory account of Vanport. Appearing as a kind of inconsequential afterthought, the last sentence contained the words, "The entire project is surrounded by an impervious dike. . . ."[1] It did seem well protected from the two areas of visible water, an island channel about a mile to the north, and on the south a dirty, narrow body of sluggish water called Columbia Slough. Except during major runoffs, water usually could not be seen from the base of the high railroad fill on the west, where the delta-like area at the confluence of the Willamette and Columbia rivers ended. Out of view were backwater lakes and marshes, and it was from here that the Columbia Slough waters originated. Denver Avenue on the east served in effect, as the first of several lateral dikes stretching eastward up the Columbia River.

In May 1948, over 6,000 of Vanport's original 9,942 units remained. There were less than a 1000 vacancies, and these were scattered throughout the project rather than being in any closed section. Later, Harry Freeman was to fix occupancy at 5,295 families containing 18,700 "actual registered tenants." Newspaper statistics varied slightly from Freeman's and also fixed the final

family ratio between white and black at 75 percent to 25 percent.[2]

As the days of May followed one another, a somewhat bedraggled Vanport went about its daily routine. An exceptionally heavy winter snowfall had accumulated in the Columbia River basin drainage area where the mighty river carried moisture from seven states and British Columbia on its way to the Pacific Ocean. There had not been an excessive amount of rain or warm weather in the early spring, either of which might have served to carry off more of the snowpack. May, however, produced a combination of warm temperatures and heavy rains throughout much of the basin, and the most water since 1894 came quickly. It surged in mainly from the Canadian Rockies, the Kootenai and Flathead rivers, and the Clearwater and Salmon rivers in Idaho.[3]

As the river began to build towards what would turn out to be a very early crest, little apprehension was felt. The minutes of the HAP commissioners' meeting on 20 May were completely routine and contained no reference of any sort to even the possible existence of a flood problem. On Tuesday, 25 May, a routine 24-hour patrol of the north and south dikes started (the only two that the water had reached). Commercial operators in the north part of the diked area assisted in the surveillance. From a road at the base of each dike one automobile, equipped with a spotlight and carrying two men with flashlights, looked for seepage, boils, or blisters. When the water reached the relatively high level of two years before, the auto patrol was increased, and a foot patrol added. No problems had developed during the 1946 flood crest. The west dike (railroad fill) was added to the patrol when the rising waters of Smith Lake reached it, and a speeder exercised a constant watch from the track itself. Sheriff Martin T. Pratt's office served to coordinate patrol communications.[4]

Housing Authority officials had decided that they would have to rely on the advice of the U.S. Army Corps of Engineers, who had completed the diking system and who had previous experience in flood control. They explained to the Corps (headed by Colonel O. E. Walsh, district engineer) the preparations they had made: 47,000 sacks of sand and 1,600 yards of loose sand stockpiled; an almost unlimited amount of baled straw; several truckloads of heavy canvas tarpaulins; a fleet of 150 trucks ready for immediate use; a standby crew of at least 50 men available on a 24-hour basis; and extensive lists of volunteers. The Engineers then informed HAP officials they had nothing to worry about.[5]

The river continued its rapid rise and now appeared more ominous. On Friday, 28 May, telephone operators at the Project Administration Building were placed on twenty-four hour duty. Sleeping quarters were prepared for key personnel and used by HAP's three top administrators. The uniform division of the Sheriff's Office went on twelve-hour shifts. Although HAP was still exhibiting outward calm, concern was being felt. A meeting to discuss the situation was held on Saturday, 29 May, at Red Cross headquarters. The possibility of evacuation was discussed. Attending were Red Cross representatives, HAP officials, a Governor's representative, one county commissioner, Sheriff Pratt, and a health department official. It was generally understood that the Army Engineers were confident there was no need for alarm.[6] However, HAP's recorded description of the meeting leaves the impression that evacuation would

have been ordered if it had been believed that housing could have been found. The Housing Authority set the number it could provide emergency housing for at 1,000–1,500, and the Red Cross at 7,500. At the outside, the possible total could be no more than 10,000, and additionally it was felt that 18,000 could not be fed either. So no decision was made, and another meeting scheduled for Monday.[7]

Vanport residents had been continually reassured that there was no danger, and as a result very few had moved. However, not every one believed all was well. A few had evacuated by Saturday. Some had moved their most desirable possessions, while still others had packed things in boxes, hooked up small trailers, and made various preparations. Relatives had evacuated some of the ill, handicapped, or disabled. One man reported occupants had been leaving all during the night (Saturday). After the Sunday, 30 May morning bulletin was delivered, a great deal of movement was noted, in spite of its assurance that there was nothing to fear.[8]

Memorial Day dawned fair and clear with a promise of more of the sunny and warm weather that had characterized May. Early that Sunday morning (4:00 A.M.) a sheet of paper bearing a message from HAP was shoved under each door by the furnace firemen. The circumstances of its genesis remained a public mystery until the trial of the flood suits, but it had been prepared by an HAP employee, John Ward, with the assistance of others, the idea having occurred as a result of the 29 May meeting at Red Cross headquarters.[9] Bitter acrimony would soon be produced by the message's reassuring tone. It stated the ". . . flood situation has not changed . . . barring unforeseen developments VANPORT is safe." However, if it should become necessary to evacuate, the ". . . Housing Authority will give warning at the earliest possible moment" by continued siren and air horn. Sound trucks would give instructions. Residents were told, if the warning came: don't panic; pack your personal belongings and a change of clothing; turn off the lights and the stove; close the windows and lock the door. If there were sick, elderly, or disabled persons, the bulletin suggested that, if it were convenient, it might be desirable for them to leave for a few days, but to be sure and register at the Sheriff's Office in case there was any inquiry. Finally the message concluded:

REMEMBER:
DIKES ARE SAFE AT PRESENT
YOU WILL BE WARNED IF NECESSARY
YOU WILL HAVE TIME TO LEAVE
DON'T GET EXCITED.[10]

During the day the temperature rose to a pleasant 76°. A heavy automobile parade of sightseers in areas adjacent to the Columbia River continued through the morning and afternoon, made up of local residents who had not left town for the holiday weekend. Fortunately, many Vanporters were also sightseeing or had joined the weekend exodus. The river gauge at Vancouver read 28.3 feet (15 feet was flood stage). At 4:00 P.M. the Corps of Engineers announced that the ground level at Vanport City was 15 feet below the level of the Columbia River and Smith Lake. Mrs. Laura Whitney, who had been at the administration building switchboard the day before constantly repeating, "There is no immediate danger. Everyone will be notified in ample time," now called in before going to work for the evening shift and was told by the on-duty operator that the dike might go at any time. Sheriff Pratt was approaching Red Cross headquarters for a special meeting on flood conditions in the Northwest area but specifically the possible evacuation of Vanport. Another meeting on the same subject was in progress at Army Engineers headquarters (the Engineers were not now so certain). Word of the break arrived at both places almost simultaneously.[11]

It had occurred where it was not particularly expected. Although the railroad fill was not built as a dike, many regarded it as the strongest link in the chain.

106

Its massive proportions led to the feeling of security. It was 125 feet wide at the base and still 75 feet in width at the top. Because of the prevailing land contours, the water had reached it last and was still 17 feet from the top of the fill when it caved in.[12]

There were many different, sometimes contradictory, reports of the break, depending on the time, and where the viewer happened to be. The railroad fill gave way at approximately 4:17 P.M. Calvin Hulbert was flying a seaplane above the tracks when the roadbed washed out. He described it as a sudden six-foot break then quickly 60 feet, and then 500 feet. A wall of water 10 feet high roared through, knocking down buildings like a bulldozer, crumbling some, and popping the walls out of others. However, he was watching the area near the break, close to the location of Vanport College. In the eastern part near Denver Avenue he could observe people bustling around trying to save their belongings. At the college approximately 30 students and faculty had been working removing records. When the dike gave way, instead of rushing to save their own personal property, they scattered throughout Vanport to spread the alarm, and as a result lost most or all of their prized personal possessions.[13]

Sheriff Pratt estimated that there was about a 10 minute warning period before effects of the water were visible. He believed the loss of life would have been terrific if it had not been for this delay which enabled every available Portland Traction Company bus to rush to the scene. Many taxis also responded. Officers on duty in Vanport had difficulty hurrying people during the time the water could not be seen.[14] One can only speculate on what might have happened if the break had occurred at night.

As the surging waves first moved in, they quickly hit the many sloughs. One report described showers of spray 50 feet high upon impact with the slough water. Then, for 35 to 40 minutes a creeping inundation occurred as the sloughs absorbed much of the water. After

The site of the original break in the railroad dike. (OHS neg. 68784)

they were filled and a sheet of water had spread over Vanport, the waves began to roll again; cars were sent careening, houses wrenched apart; the water reached the high part of the project near Denver Avenue, and all vehicular traffic was quickly flooded out. Now the water level rose rapidly. Between 5:00 P.M. and 6:45 P.M. the Willamette River flood gauge dropped three inches during the massive run-off into Vanport. Then it quickly rose

At the start of the flood, water poured into the low spots of Vanport, giving a little extra time. This is a view of Force Street and the shopping center on Victory Boulevard. (OHS neg. 58665)

another six inches by 8:00 P.M. All electric power went off at 4:50 P.M. Buildings floated like slow moving giants, sometimes turning in the whirlpools being created. The water surrounded the two KGW towers, and the station left the air at 5:21. At 5:50 P.M. a floating apartment crashed into one of the towers and toppled it. The American flag on top of the project's flagpole survived until 5:44, when it was hit by a house and gently dipped into the water. Some abandoned cars with closed windows floated for a short period of time before sinking.[15]

The extreme confusion resulted in the lack of accurate, comprehensive eyewitness accounts. Bob Clark, an *Oregonian* staff writer who was at home in Vanport with his family of six when the flood hit, commented that he should have been a trained observer but instead got confused by events. One thing that all seemed to agree on was the lack of panic and the universal concern for the safety of children. While the sloughs were still absorbing the water, Portland Traction Company buses seemed to be everywhere. An unusual feature was the quiet, which seemed so strange. The cars were still lined up, bumper to bumper, when a wave of water, appearing like a fog, washed over them and flattened out. From that point on, human chains, rope chains, and boat rescue were used. Floating telephone poles and parking-lot logs proved particularly hazardous. Water in the moving apartments did not reach too high into the second floor, and here, in addition to roof tops, many

A view of Vanport and Denver Avenue shortly after the break in the railroad dike. Note the buses loading residents at the Denver Avenue approach. (OHS neg. 24149)

109

A few hours after the break. There are fewer buses, but notice people in row-boats. (OHS neg. 68803)

people found a haven. A man was seen paddling on a floating mattress. Some residents who were in other parts of Vanport tried to return to their homes, and when the water got too deep to wade, grabbed planks, logs, or other debris and attempted to pole or paddle their way.[16]

110

By the time Sheriff Pratt reached Vanport City after fighting his way through the traffic, the water was beginning to lap at the Denver Avenue fill. People were still being taken from the water. He immediately issued an emergency call for boats, and many arrived quickly. As the water continued to rise children were tossed into the boats from upper floor windows. Soon the boats could take people directly from the roofs and upper floors. One officer observed a very drunk man get out of a boat at the base of Denver Avenue near the north approach to Vanport, and before anyone could stop him he jumped back into the water and swam to a floating apartment building about 100 feet away. What happened to him after that was unknown. The compactness of the project and its proximity to Denver Avenue proved to be invaluable assets. Buses, taxis, ambulances, and private cars wishing to assist lined the thoroughfare. Operations were somewhat hindered by long lines of sightseers on all the surrounding roads.[17]

The Sheriff's Office established emergency headquarters at the Denver Avenue exit to Vanport, while the Multnomah County Health Department and the American Red Cross set up emergency stations nearby. However, during the first two hours, the health department

Cars trying to get out of Vanport. Most of these cars never made it due to congestion at the entrance to Vanport. This picture was taken about 45 minutes after the break. (OHS neg. 53265)

This human chain served as a lifeline for the last people out of Vanport. (OHS neg. 52428)

station treated only about a dozen people for minor injuries. As evening approached more systematic operations began to take place. Organized searching turned up a few more people in upper-floor apartments. One couple was trapped as the house tipped crazily and sealed off the door and windows. Men on a boat chopped a hole in the wall in order to save them. As night descended floodlights powered by portable generators illuminated part of the area, along with fire department searchlights. By 9:00 P.M. the search crews believed no one was still marooned.[18]

The Oregon National Guard arrived, bringing four new amphibious "Buffaloes." It had been activated by Governor John H. Hall immediately upon receiving word of the disaster. Two hundred men were mobilized and on the scene by 10:00 P.M., and several hundred more were expected by morning. With the coming of the Guard the area became effectively patrolled, and looting was stopped. There had been few reports of looting, but Sheriff Pratt believed some did occur during the period of the emergency boat call and continued on until all unauthorized boats could be kept out. That same evening the Interstate Bridge was closed to general traffic in order to facilitate emergency work, and many Vancouver residents coming home that Sunday evening from long drives to the Oregon beaches and other areas faced a 100 mile detour. By midnight not a single fatality had been discovered. Brick chimneys

112

stood starkly alone in the water that was now fifteen feet deep. The apartment buildings floated eerily, but they were tending to pile up, along with other assorted flotsam and jetsam, against the Denver Avenue fill.[19]

At daylight an overall search plan was put into operation. Broken upper floor windows signified that a building had been searched. In one second story apartment a newspaper lay open to the headline "Crest Due Tuesday," in another an uncarved beef roast and bowl of mashed potatoes sat on the dinner table in front of the pushed-back chairs. No bodies were discovered. As the "Buffaloes" hunted for the dead, a newspaper reporter thought of the theme that had been selected a week earlier for the Vanport float in Portland's Rose Festival. It was "Water Babies."[20]

As Monday wore on, some apprehension developed in regard to the Denver Avenue fill. Sheriff Martin T. Pratt moved his temporary headquarters to the intersection of Union and Vancouver Avenues. At approximately 9:30 P.M., as a Portland General Electric Company

Standing on the roof of a Vanport apartment, two men attempt to salvage their belongings as they float by. (OHS neg. 68808)

Residents of Vanport fleeing from the flood waters. Photographer Mel Junghans. (OHS neg. CN 006190)

emergency vehicle carrying a lone occupant traveled over Denver Avenue, the road collapsed, and the vehicle disappeared beneath the waters, bringing the first certain fatality. One hundred men had worked at the spot all day, and it was felt that it would hold. Soon the break widened to 500 feet, and the apartment buildings began floating through, slowly and majestically, at times several abreast. Before long the area east of Denver Avenue (now occupied by Portland Meadows Race Track, several stores, fast-food establishments, and a Portland public park) was well populated with them.[21]

The Red Cross had quickly established a downtown Portland emergency headquarters. Within one-half hour after the water started pouring into Vanport the first refugees appeared. Greyhound buses that had now joined the transport effort soon began unloading them in a steady stream.[22] Because of the previous assurances of no danger and the short warning period, the refugees

113

Noon the day after the flood. Notice Mt. St. Helens in the background. (OHS neg. 68818)

had been able to save very few of their belongings. Fortunately for them, the complete furnishing of the apartments by the government, the rules about removing any of the contents, and the small size of the quarters helped to hold down the accumulation of bulky material goods.

An effective organizational operation to meet the emergency needs sprang into action. Radio appeals were made for needed food and clothing, which were to be brought to the several grade schools that were to be used for emergency housing. At Camp Clatsop (Astoria, Oregon) volunteers loaded cots and bedding on 30 National Guard trucks. Offers of emergency housing in private homes were solicited. Registration of refugees began at tables placed on the sidewalk at the down-

Amphibious vehicles were used in searching for any remaining survivors. Photo by Russ Allemang. (OHS neg. 68768)

Vanport's float in the 1948 Rose Festival. The theme of the float was "Water Babies." (OHS neg. 68807)

town headquarters and at the Portland Armory, where National Guardsmen aided Red Cross workers in the task. A quickly organized cafeteria started serving plates of spaghetti.[23]

As the refugees arrived at the schools, thousands were taken away into private homes. For example, of the 321 persons registered at Ockley Green School only 17 slept there, and eight of these were in one family where a measles quarantine existed. In addition to the eight grade schools, Roosevelt and Jefferson High schools were also used. Approximately 100 slept at the Williams Avenue YMCA (Young Men's Christian Association); and 1,000 were divided between the Jewish Community Center, the Portland Armory, and American Legion Post Number 1. Many churches remained open. Soon there was more temporary housing than was needed. The color line disappeared as black Vanporters were taken into white homes. School staffs reported for emergency work. Neighbors in school areas brought pots of coffee and sandwiches until cafeterias were operating. The Red Cross discovered it could feed those remaining at the schools, armory, and other centers from its own supplies. By Tuesday, 1 June, Roosevelt and Jefferson High Schools were no longer needed.[24] It was the traditional American response to disaster.

One out of every ten people appearing at Red Cross headquarters had suffered family separation during the

The Red Cross moved into action quickly to help the survivors. This photo was taken the day after the flood. Photo by Walter M. Hippler. (OHS neg. 60378)

plane. Eventually a phone clearance depot was established at Jefferson High School by school officials. Gradually families became reunited.[25]

Meanwhile, other steps were being taken to handle immediate or anticipated problems. Grocery stores in North Portland rescinded the scheduled Monday holiday closing. Immunization clinics for those who had swallowed Columbia River water were opened on Monday. An announcement was made to families who had taken in refugees that if anyone became ill with an infectious disease he could be taken to Portland's Isolation Hospital. President Truman declared Vanport a disaster area and ordered the use of surplus war property for relief and rehabilitation, in addition to authorizing the distribution of some army and navy materials.[26]

As the days passed the Red Cross continued its operations, and the Multnomah County Sheriff's Office

The Red Cross established a downtown emergency headquarters on SW 15th and Alder Street. Buses unloaded Vanport refugees in a steady stream. Photo by Walter M. Hippler. (OHS neg. 60370)

evacuation. There were pitiful scenes as individuals tried to locate relatives. Some cried openly while others sat on the pavement in a stony silence. Residents of Vanport who were away from the town when the flood hit desperately tried to find out what had happened to their loved ones. Among these were several members of the Portland Beavers baseball team which was playing in Seattle (five wives and seven children were in Vanport, including the wife and child of Mayo Smith, later to become the manager of the world champion Detroit Tigers). Bill Mulligan, the team's general manager, who was in Portland, rushed to Vanport when he heard of the flood, was let through police lines, but in the confusion could find no trace of the missing wives and children. He immediately wired the players to charter a special worked with it in locating people and coordinating communications. On Tuesday, 1 June, the Columbia crested at 30.2 feet and began a long, slow drop. The Sheriff's Office continued with whatever needed to be done at the site of flooded Vanport. Some frictions arose. In a letter thanking the Sea Scouts for their splendid work, Sheriff Martin T. Pratt contrasted it to his experience with the United States Coast Guard. During the first few days after the inundation there was a great need for officially marked boats. Pratt went to the Coast Guard headquarters at McCuddy's Moorage on the Oregon side of the Columbia River. There he was told by a moorage official that the Coast Guard had pulled their boats out of the water and left—he thought for some place on Columbia Boulevard. Finally, Pratt located the boats. They were parked on trailers on the lawn at Broadmoor Golf Course with the ". . . men lounging around doing nothing. . . ." He was told by a Coast Guard officer that their regulations forbade them from doing any civilian police work. So the Sheriff left in disgust. Later the boats appeared on the waters at Vanport, but there was no liaison work. Pratt stated that he did not know what they did, and rather caustically remarked, ". . . they may have saved a few cats, dogs, chickens. . . ." The Coast Guard did find one body and removed it from the scene instead of bringing it to the coroner's depot at the landing. Pratt attributed the whole trouble to bureaucratic organizational inflexibility, rather than to the men involved.[27]

The most pressing problem was a more permanent solution of the housing needs of displaced Vanporters. The American Red Cross was well aware that the refugees' welcome in strangers' homes would wear out quickly. Although it had never before been faced with a housing problem of this magnitude, it was willing to help but felt it was primarily a community responsibility. The community, however, was somewhat divided on how to proceed. One of the county commissioners

Mrs. Lizzie Phillips and her children, Cleaven and Esther May, were among many thousands evacuated from Vanport. They were under Red Cross care at the Portland Armory. (OHS neg. 61319)

wanted the Red Cross to take the initiative. The Portland Realty Board wished the problem solved through private housing. A Vanport College official declared that many veterans had had faith in the siren system, and as a result did not leave quickly enough to save many of their belongings, so the federal government should provide direct aid.[28]

Although it might have eschewed responsibility, HAP stepped into the breach. With the aid of other federal agencies it was responsible for what was done. Because it had less than 500 vacancies in its other projects, $50,000,000 was requested for permanent housing to replace that which was lost. Only $10,000,000 was re-

117

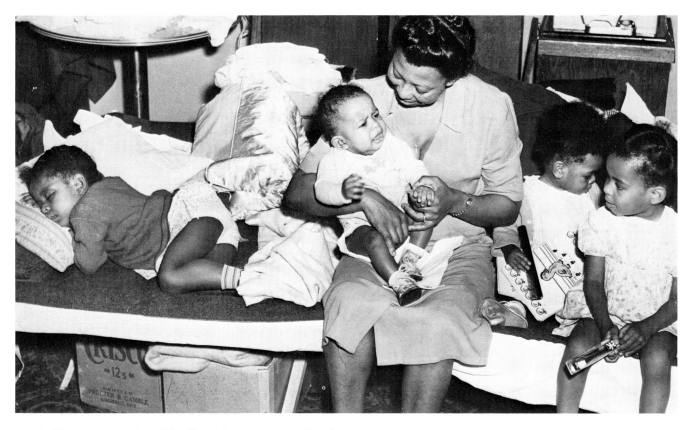

Flood refugees Mrs. Edna Tidwell and her youngsters found a temporary home at the Portland American Legion Post No. 1. (OHS neg. 78695)

ceived and that for emergency use. To meet the immediate need, federal trailers were imported and installed at several locations. Many of these had seen heavy wartime use and were in poor condition, resulting in HAP taking some severe, rather unjust criticism. These trailers, augmented later by some of better quality, served to house the vast bulk of the refugees who were without resources of their own.[29]

As late as 24 July the Red Cross was still operating one shelter at Swan Island. The number there had stabilized at about 1,325. It required approximately $8,000 per week to feed them. Another problem encountered by refugees was that some insurance companies would not make settlements on cars until they were recovered from the water, and as late as 11 August, some had not been recovered.[30]

The sudden flood made the front page of newspapers all over the United States. *Newsweek* compared it to the Johnstown flood of 31 May 1899. As a result, a great number of requests for information poured in from concerned relatives elsewhere in the country. Soon letters bearing donations and messages of concern

118

Two victims of the flood try to make themselves as comfortable as possible in the garage of a friend. (OHS neg. 68989)

Carl Downey carrying unidentified woman to safety. He rescued her from the roof top in the background and wended his way across the plywood plank walkway others laid on top of the floatsam. The woman was too frightened to give her name. Photo by Mel Junghans. (OHS neg. 78870)

for the refugees began to be received from many areas of the United States and from Scotland, England, and the Netherlands. They came from individuals, churches, schools, and cities. Two Mississippi towns sent more than $3,000. A city in the Netherlands promised to send art objects which could be sold. It was their way of extending a helping hand in appreciation for United States help in rebuilding their country after World War II. Over $500 came from patrons of the Bowery Cafe in Hamtramck, Michigan, and University of Washington students collected $1,000. Governor Thomas E. Dewey of New York offered Governor John H. Hall of Oregon any assistance his state could give.[31]

As the water settled in and covered Vanport City, rumors flew. Martin T. Pratt described them as "terrible." Stewart Holbrook, in an article which later appeared in the *New Yorker*, used them as a basis for some

Refugees crowded Red Cross registration tables as an attempt was made to compile a list of missing persons. (OHS neg. 68990)

pungent observations on rumor-spreading. One of the first was that a large number of children had been trapped in the theater and perished there. It was not until 3 June, that this story was laid to rest by a denial in the Portland *Oregonian*. Another had a school bus loaded with children caught by the first wave, and after the water had stabilized, 50 people had seen the submerged bus with heads, arms, and legs sticking out of the windows. A third told of the secret loading in the dead of night of 457 bodies on a ship bound for Japan. Eventually they were to be returned as dead soldiers. The reason for this ploy was to cover up responsibility for the lack of adequate warning. Perhaps the most damaging story, and one which may have helped create some of the others, was a statement actually attributed to city and county officials. It declared the lower floors of the apartment buildings were "clogged with hun-

dreds of bodies," that many had been swept into the main river and from there out to sea, and thus the exact count of dead would never be known. But the rumor that spread the farthest and fastest was one that originated when a woman called all her friends, telling them she had seen a room in a Portland cold storage plant containing at least 600 bodies. In this one, the reason given for secrecy was to minimize the magnitude of the disaster until after the Portland Rose Festival celebration.[32]

It would be months before the official death toll could be determined. Two bodies reportedly were seen on the day of the break by the looting patrol, but the water was still rising, and they could not be gotten out. Over 2,000 names were on the missing list. Amidst all the apprehension and rumors Sheriff Pratt predicted the toll with almost uncanny accuracy. He estimated it would not be more than 25, based on his evaluation of

120

officers' reports, the lack of hysteria, the three-day holi-day, the 35 to 40 minutes it took the sloughs to fill, and the time of day (Sunday P.M.). Another helpful factor was the progress in phasing out Vanport Hospital. By 1 May, all bed patients had been moved to Kaiser's Vancouver hospital, and the out-patient clinic closed on Sundays. In the face of criticism Pratt stubbornly stuck to his prediction. Richard L. Neuberger (later U.S.

Union Ave. (lower left) emerges from the waters in front of the Amphi-theatre. Beyond, Portland Raceway bleachers rise with the Portland Meadows Horse Track Grandstand in the distance. (OHS neg. 68989)

The Terminal Ice and Cold Storage Company, rumored to contain the bodies of a secret 600 flood victims. Photo by Walter M. Hippler. (OHS neg. 60392)

Senator from Oregon), in an article appearing in *The Nation* 13 days after the flood, gave a figure of 200 as an estimate from the local coroner's office.[33]

The river receded ever so slowly, and Vanport was not completely uncovered for many weeks. After about five days the first bodies were recovered. Only 13 had been found by 10 September. Eventually the Multnomah County Coroner's official list of bodies recovered was set at 15 with the acknowledgment that there may have been other victims whose bodies were never discovered. On 23 June, the Red Cross submitted to Sheriff Pratt a list of 18 names of people residing in Vanport whose relatives were trying to locate them, stated it had exhausted its resources, and it must be presumed that some had died in the flood. Seven of these were never located. Although there were many transients in Vanport, probably at least some of these seven lost their lives, and their bodies were carried into the main river and perhaps from there to the ocean or some other unknown fate.[34]

122

As the immediate emergency subsided, individual reactions of Vanport citizens varied. One family saw the hand of the Lord in their escape and published a small booklet on their experiences. They saw in the catastrophe ". . . a fresh realization of the need to prepare and continually watch for the sudden coming of our Lord." Upon cramming their belongings in a small trailer readied for a possible emergency, they suddenly discovered that the car keys were in another pair of pants in the bottom of the trailer. As the members of a patrol truck cursed them for blocking the road, a screwdriver lying on the floor of the car was used in the ignition, and miraculously, the car started. The Lord fulfilled his promise by not only saving them, but their car, trailer, and much of their earthly goods. However, He did not do as well for two elderly ladies in their congregation who died in their crushed apartment.[35]

Many Vanporters were bitter over the shortness of the warning, and one resident maintained twenty minutes was the most that anyone had. Henry L. Doeneka, chief engineer at Multnomah County Hospital for 25 years, was especially critical and did not mind speaking for publication. According to him, the siren was not heard in the southeast section. Residents there lost almost everything. The only officers seen were two deputy sheriffs who were running, one with his uniform under his arm. They said nothing, and the water came 10 minutes later. There was no traffic direction, and three lanes formed on the two-lane street. Meanwhile, Denver Avenue was allowed to plug up, trapping cars in the project. He blamed the loss of lives and property on the Housing Authority, who had assured the residents over and over again of orderly evacuation if necessary—even telling a neighbor that all was well 20 minutes before the water came.[36]

One facet that did not get thoroughly aired in the public controversy was the circumstances surrounding the warning of the break, possibly because of the question of legal liability. The *Oregonian* first reported that an amateur shortwave radio operator at the scene of the break flashed the warning before fleeing, and that his message—plus the shouts of others—alerted the operator of the warning siren, who then gave the signal.[37] This account actually was incorrect. Later stories were somewhat more accurate but still lacked important details.

The *Oregonian* and Oregon *Journal* requested copies of Sheriff's officers' reports on events at the time of the break, but they apparently acceded to Sheriff Pratt's suggestion that some of the contents remain confidential because of undecided legal questions. Information had been obtained by an investigating officer from a Floyd V. Wright, who was operating a speeder patrolling the railroad fill. When the roadbed gave way, within a period of a very few minutes he had run his speeder to the stockyards and contacted W.E. Williams, president of Portland Union Stockyards, in his office. Williams, who could see the break from his office windows, immediately called Harry D. Jaeger, Vanport City manager, at the Vanport headquarters at 4:17 P.M. He told whoever took the call that the west wall had broken and to alert the people. They waited for awhile and did not hear the siren. Finally, Williams called again and said, "for God's sake alert those people." Shortly afterwards the siren went off.[38]

The Housing Authority of Portland, undoubtedly

The extent of the damage and wreckage caused by the flood. (OHS neg. 8445)

123

anticipating possible criticism or worse in view of all its previous assurances of no danger, hurriedly issued a kind of "white paper" the day following the flood. It elaborately detailed their preparations and precautions, but differed significantly in the description of events surrounding the giving of the warning. According to it, when Williams called he spoke to Roy W. Taylor, assistant director, management division HAP, and said, "We have a bad break in the railroad fill near the northwest corner of the project and it looks very bad. It's flowing through a gap of approximately 50 feet, and if all men, materials, and equipment are gotten there quickly we may be able to stop it." Jaeger then got into his car, went to the northwestern area of the project near the stockyards, and told the supervisor of the transportation and labor crews to move all men, materials, and equipment to the break area. Harry D. Freeman stayed with the phone while Taylor went 50 feet down the hall, where he ordered a standby crew of about 40 men to the site of the break. Taylor then notified an electrician to stand by in case it became necessary to activate the warning siren and returned to his office. At that point he received the second call from Williams to the effect that the break had widened to 100 feet, and the alarm should be given. He reported this to Freeman who then issued the order to start the siren.[39]

To prevent relay burn-out, the siren system had to be controlled manually with intermittent starts and stops. Finally, an electrician shorted the wiring for continual operation. Taylor climbed on the roof from where he could see the waves coming across the field in the northwest corner. Everyone in the building was told to get out. Jaeger came back from the break, reporting it to be hopeless. The officials then left, Jaeger and Taylor returning to the dike break and deciding again that there was no hope.[40]

Of course the crux of the matter was what Williams said over the phone in his first call, there being two contradictory reports, one by Wright who was listening in

Williams' office and one by Taylor who was taking the call. In addition to Taylor's version in the HAP report there was some variation in the newspaper stories that appeared two days after the flood, in which certain descriptions of the conversation were ascribed to Taylor and to Mrs. Taylor. In one *Oregonian* story Taylor was described as being at the phone when Williams' first call came, and the alarm was sounded "within a matter of seconds," and a sandbag crew sent on the way. Another story in the same paper the same day quoted Mrs. Taylor's second-hand account, one which was perhaps slightly embellished but possibly a better description of the situation. According to her, Williams suddenly broke off the conversation with, "The dike's going out!" Then Taylor hung up, sent two cars to investigate, but before they got back Williams called again, stating, "It's a bad break. You can't stop it. Get the people out." The siren was then sounded.[41] Unfortunately, no account by Williams is available. Another matter skipped over or conveniently ignored was whether any adequate testing of the sirens had been done. From the difficulties encountered it appeared not.

After passions had subsided a little, Bob Clark, an *Oregonian* staff writer living in Vanport, offered some constructive criticism and comment. Who decided, he asked, on one exit for 40,000 people, or even 18,500? Booster groups had been interested mainly in industry, not in the living conditions of employees. During the inundation, traffic policemen had tried their best, but the job was impossible. One of the most poignant, heart-rending aspects of the flood was the lineup of cars on Denver Avenue, full of children, unable to move because of the traffic congestion, and thus the children were forced to watch the destruction of all their cherished possessions, after their parents, depending on HAP advice, had continually assured them that there was nothing to fear.[42] No warning of the desirability of moving any belongings was ever given.

Responsibility in connection with the disaster re-

Many children watched as their homes were destroyed. (OHS neg. 1526)

mained a thorny and tangled question. The government loss of an estimated $21,500,000 in property was perhaps unavoidable, but if the project had been evacuated for a week during the high water period, no lives would have been lost, and the utterly incalculable loss of prized personal possessions avoided. The several thousand who were away from home that Sunday afternoon lost any piece of their past that was subject to water damage. Those in Vanport, who, when the alarm sounded, turned to helping others, discovered too late that they could salvage nothing of their own.[43]

As in most disasters people quickly looked for scapegoats, real or imagined, and there were only two possibilities, HAP and the Army Corps of Engineers. The Housing Authority of Portland immediately, in the public press, took the position that it had done all it possibly could, and if there was any blame it must be assigned to the Corps of Engineers. Their attorney, Lester W. Humphreys, was quoted, "The housing authority feels terribly, terribly bad that lives possibly were lost, but all you can do is depend on the advice of competent engineers." Chairman Herbert J. Dahlke openly criticized the district engineers, declaring their office had relied entirely upon them and the two experts the engineers had brought in, experts who had been present when the diking system was completed. Dahlke claimed he would have pushed for evacuation in spite of the engineers, except he had been repeatedly assured by them that any break-through would be a matter of hours.[44]

The Housing Authority continued its defense. Despite assurances from the engineers, HAP had made their few plans for evacuation in a meeting at Red Cross headquarters the day preceding the flood. Two sirens and a sound truck were readied, and a man stationed at the alarm on a 24-hour basis. Portland Traction Company went on a standby basis, ready to provide buses for evacuation. The dike was inspected Saturday at 10:30 P.M. by the engineers, accompanied by Executive Director Harry D. Freeman, City Manager Harold Jaeger, and Dahlke. They were again assured by the engineers that it was in good shape, growing tighter "like a barrel."[45]

In defense, the United States Army Corps of Engineers recounted the history of diking in the area. The railroad fill had survived a similar situation in 1933. In 1941, the whole system was completed and turned over to Peninsula Diking District Number 1. As the flood danger appeared the engineers had called in two expert trouble-shooters, and sand-bagging operations were conducted, but there had been no seepage around the railroad fill. Colonel Orville E. Walsh maintained that, although the district engineer experts had advised the Housing Authority the area looked safe, they had never made any statement that justified the tone of the Sunday morning circular.[46]

A theory as to the cause of the break in the railway fill quickly appeared. From about 1907 to 1918 the railroad in that area had run over the lowlands on a long trestle . When the fill was made the trestle was left, and

125

aggregate simply dumped into the area surrounding it. The passage of time rotted the timbers, weakening the roadbed at that point. Albert S. Witchell, the retired chief railroad engineer for the Spokane, Portland, and Seattle Railroad confirmed the relevant facts.[47] Whether the theory was correct or not remained another matter.

The Housing Authority's attempt to place all the blame squarely upon the Army Engineers was not a total success. In their bitterness, Vanport residents did enough mud-slinging to touch every administrative group involved in Vanport. Advocates of permanent public housing used the refugee housing problem as a further argument in their attack on HAP as representing private housing interests. Both of the area's major newspapers joined in the attack which eventually resulted in significant changes in the board of commissioners in 1949. In his mid-June article in *The Nation*, Richard Neuberger called the performance of the Army Engineers an example of bureaucratic bungling, and the excuse that because the railroad fill was built many years ago they did not know of the rotting timbers was simply not adequate. The Oregon State Grange, interested in a regional Columbia Valley Authority rather than piecemeal operation by the Bonneville Power Administration, Bureau of Reclamation, and Army Engineers, charged the engineers were unfit to hold their positions. Enraged citizens searched for any target on which to vent their spleen. In retrospect some of the charges appear humorous, but were not considered so at the time. The Sheriff's Office received the butt of much criticism and it reported that, one of the accusers ". . . who has taken somewhat of an indifferent attitude toward our organization during this flood disaster," charged them with shooting beaver at the scene, when they were in fact shooting at a rat. Three weeks after the disaster, a citizens' committee representing Vanport refugees was appealing to the Portland City Council for help not only in obtaining additional housing, but for job priorities and stop-gap spending money as well.[48]

126

Unquestionably, HAP did rely and operate on the advice of the U.S. Army Corps of Engineers, and the Engineers were willing and desirous of being in this position of responsibility. However, as previously mentioned, the 29 May meeting did consider the possibility of evacuation. Apparently what held back the decision to evacuate, in addition to the evaluation of the flood possibility by the engineers, was the magnitude of the housing problem. After the flood HAP maintained the total decision was based on assurances from the engineers, not a completely frank recounting. Certainly Col. O. E. Walsh's argument that the information furnished by the engineers did not merit the tone of the Sunday morning circular had considerable validity. In fact, during the later damage trials, U.S. government attorneys were anxious to have the details of responsibility for the circular kept secret until they could make their own presentation. The Vanport flood became, as with many catastrophes, something for which it was almost impossible to assess blame, but, with benefit of hindsight, it was possible to point to a place where a slight shifting of judgments might have avoided the loss of life and cherished possessions.

There were many other ramifications of the flood. An abrupt announcement the following day said Vanport College was being indefinitely discontinued. Spring term examinations for its 1,265 students were cancelled. The school's library was a total loss. Fortunately, a group of volunteers using two school buses and a truck saved much of the light office equipment, laboratory equipment, and the all-important student files. As the emergency period closed, the Oregon National Guard and Sheriff's Reserve left the long term search for bodies and the prevention of looting to the Multnomah County Sheriff's office.[49]

The Housing Authority immediately took charge of salvage operations upon "verbal approval" of higher federal housing officials. At first not too much could be done. Eleven amphibious vehicles were obtained and proceeded to recover what they could. Material was tagged and placed in two warehouses. Listings were published in the newspapers by apartment number and tenant. Individuals could claim their possessions by identifying themselves. They then had to provide transportation for the goods. Vanport merhants were allowed to employ their own divers, after first obtaining HAP approval. Towards the end of June the FPHA Regional Office ordered HAP to discontinue its salvage activity because there was no authority for the use of federal housing funds to pay the cost ($1,500 a day at that time). Harry Freeman objected strenuously and was told to call the National Commissioner in Washington, D.C. The commissioner authorized continuance, saying they would decide later how to legally obtain the funds for salvaging tenant belongings. Although the Army Engineers recovered the post office safe, the United States Post Office Department had to hope that later operations would turn up missing sacks of mail and C.O.D. packages. A shingle company was allowed to round up hundreds of bundles of shingles that had floated through the break.[50]

At the end of June, 120 apartment buildings were still unidentified because of the remaining water. By this time many Vanporters had returned to their previous place of residence. Many were probably never able to recover their belongings, even if they were eventually found and sent to a warehouse. Almost two months passed before the water left the roads and the cleanup could really get under way. Under certain conditions former tenants were allowed a further search for their belongings. The apartment building must have been located, and a pass obtained. Then a colored flag was put on the tenant's car and he was accompanied by an HAP inspector. Even so, looters managed to get in. Sheriff's deputies were instructed to yell at trespassers twice, then fire a warning shot. Ex-residents had approximately a month to reclaim any on-site property. On 30 July, HAP placed an advertisement in the local papers notifying

A jumble of floating but identified apartment buildings. (OHS neg. 68992)

tenants everything must be removed by August 16. Another notice appeared on 21 August, announcing demolition would start on 23 August.[51]

The contract was awarded to a local firm, Zidell Machinery Company. As it started work during the last week of August, water still surrounded the Vanport Extension Center buildings and the State of Oregon had not as yet been able to salvage its property. By mid-December the job was about one-third completed. Even as the vestigial remains of Vanport disappeared it held its news value. *Newsweek* called it ". . . one of the biggest salvage jobs in the nation's history" and reported a foreman's story about a rumor that a worker had uncovered $3,000 and for days afterwards, instead of wreckers, the company had "treasure hunters" at $1.70 an hour. There were contractual difficulties over meeting the completion deadline, whether the cleanup had been adequately done, and the final financial settlement.[52] On 30 April 1949, with the clean-up practically complete, the last 42 assorted buildings were sold for whatever they would bring. At the first auctions some of the apartment buildings had brought as much as $2,500. On this day the crowd was small, and the first one sold for $425.[53] Thus the material remains of Vanport disappeared into history.

From the day of the disaster practically everyone realized that liability for the losses was going to be an important and difficult question. On 1 June 1948, (two days following the flood) the *Oregonian* carried advice to ex-residents from a Portland attorney to the effect that they make lists of losses because of the possibility of federal liability or Congressional action.[54] Awareness of possible liability must also have been a factor in the statement issued by HAP immediately following the flood outlining its role in the actions taken. Previous mention has been made of Sheriff Pratt's suggestion to two newspaper editors that they be careful what they use from officers' reports. Many suits were quickly filed, and many more were being threatened.[55]

On 2 November HAP held a special meeting to consider the problem of the suits. It did carry some insurance with private companies. However, the amount was trivial in relation to the loss of life and personal injury and did not even cover property damage. The insurance contained a stipulation that the insurance company could not raise government immunity as a defense without the consent of the insured (HAP). According to the applicable federal manual of procedure HAP was not to give its consent without prior approval from federal authorities. This approval had been secured but only for property loss, not for death or personal injury claims. The Housing Authority felt this was a very inconsistent position, and its attorney, Lester Humphreys, believed

Harold Makin in diving suit, descends into murky waters flowing through the break in Denver Ave. (OHS neg. 78868)

128

Mr. and Mrs. Jack Lucas. At the time this photo was taken they were living with Mrs. Lucas' mother while building a house of their own, chiefly from Vanport wreckage. (OHS neg. 78871)

HAP could legally permit the underwriters to use the defense without federal approval, but it was not advisable because the federal authorities might consider it a breach of the lease. So HAP decided that since the insurance did not cover property damage, HAP itself should use governmental immunity as a defense, and, additionally, it should be applied to loss of life and personal injury claims, and their insurers should also be permitted to use this defense. It authorized its attorney and one of the commissioners (Lamar Tooze, who also hap-

pened to be a lawyer) to go to Washington, D.C. to confer with the Legal Department of the Public Housing Administration. Approval apparently was secured.[56] In protecting its own position HAP thus provided a considerable bonus to the underwriters.

The action then shifted to the courts. As HAP was a state agency the first group of suits (165 for $445,000 property damage plus nine death and two personal injury claims) was decided in an Oregon state court. Since they were acting in a governmental capacity, HAP filed a demurrer of immunity, and the court decided for them.[57] This ended the attempt to collect damages from HAP or the insurers. The scene then moved to the federal courts because under a federal tort claims law the United States permitted itself to be sued and did not claim governmental immunity.

The Congress of the United States set August 1950 as the deadline for the filing of suits. By that time there were over 700 cases (approximately 650 involving the Vanport site—the others from nearby inundated areas) involving 2,993 claimants and 91 attorneys. All claimants had to stipulate they would abide by the decision rendered for a typical 20-case selection. Judge James Alger Fee, in whose court the trials got under way on 6 August 1951, regarded the cases as "cutting new ground." In an attempt to prove negligence, the plaintiffs established that a crack 60 feet long had appeared on top of the railroad fill three days before the break. The defense countered with testimony from a Southern California water district engineer that such a crack did not necessarily mean anything. In general the plaintiffs took the tack that their clients planned to move out but they were allayed by the reassurances of the Sunday morning bulletin. Judge Fee then made a finding that negligence was not involved, and the basis of any liability must lay in government ownership of the land.[58]

During the plaintiffs' presentation Judge Fee tried unsuccessfully to determine the relevant facts in regard

The remains of Vanport towards the end of the salvage operation. (OHS neg. 37950)

to the authorship of the bulletin and the decision to circulate it. Only the defense had these facts and they were able to hold them back until their case was presented. It was finally disclosed that the bulletin idea had come out of the 29 May meeting at Red Cross headquarters. John L. Ward (HAP project services manager) was authorized to prepare and circulate it because HAP had the resources for preparation and delivery. The defense held that Title 33 of the judicial code clearly stated that the government shall not be held responsible for flood damage. Judge Fee agreed, and the plaintiffs lost all cases.[59]

In the whole process of liability the tenant got little consideration. Understandably HAP was concerned with the possibility that liability judgments might threaten its very existence. So it wanted assurance from federal authorities that any damages awarded that exceeded insurance coverage would be paid from federal funds.[60] This federal officials refused to do and at first authorized use of governmental immunity but not for death or personal injury claims. Unwilling to take the chance (on behalf of the tenant) that federal appropriations to cover death and injury awards might later be forthcoming, HAP used the governmental immunity defense for all claims. When it did, the United States Government voiced no overt objection. The Housing Authority's attitude toward tenant losses was at times quite cavalier. A tenant, who had properly identified his belongings in unit 6404, returned some days later to get them. When he found them gone he was told by HAP that it was too bad but there was nothing they could do, the building was now under contract to Zidell Machinery Company.[61]

Unquestionably, in the federal court trial, Judge Fee was legally on firm ground once he ruled out the question of negligence. Yet, the concept of equity seemingly would have called for some compensation, perhaps through Congressional appropriation. Admittedly administration would have been difficult. But federal approval was given for locating Vanport where it was, a state agency administered it under federal direction, and another federal agency (Corps of Engineers) supervised flood control. All were responsible for assuring Vanporters there was no danger, and as a result thousands of people suffered property loss, and some were injured or even lost their life. Essentially the only defense offered to deny civil damages to people like Frederick Kinser, who swam three hours in the flood and suffered multiple injuries that made him unable to work for sixteen months,[62] was that an honest mistake had been made, and the government agencies were not liable under the law. Even the industries on the north side of what had once been Vanport were unable to obtain any reimbursement for the money they had spent trying to save the dikes. All of this presents a picture in rather sharp contrast to the attitude of government and the courts today.[63]

By the time Judge Fee rendered his decision in October 1952, the refugee housing problem had passed from public view. Former Vanporters had either left the area or found other permanent public or private housing. The temporary trailer courts were gone. With the final denial of legal responsibility Vanport disappeared into oblivion.

Could a rampaging Columbia River again inundate its diked plain? According to the Army Engineers the answer was no. The buried trestle was an unknown factor that cannot be repeated. No other main dike in the area has ever broken. Besides, there are now fourteen major dams on the Columbia River system, and they can store 10,000,000 acre feet of water. By coupling this storage ability with advanced river forecasting, aided by computers, a 1967 forecast crest of over 26.5 feet was held to 21.5 feet and kept there for 20 days. The United States and Canada were adding three dams each. Then a Vanport flood could be held to 24 feet instead of 30, and the record flood of 1894 to 26 feet. Still, in May 1972, with a record snowpack in the mountains, the Engineers were planning to seal off Columbia Slough and were reinforcing the railroad grade.[64]

The people apparently believed it could happen again. Although sentiment was perhaps swinging to some permanent form of occupancy at the time of the flood, it was never really considered afterwards. Various plans for utilization by industry never got anywhere. Many people felt that, except for the loss of life and possessions, the flood was providential in that it eliminated what would have become a difficult problem. Ownership reverted from FPHA to the Public Housing Administration in Washington D.C. For seven years, what had once been the site of the largest housing project in the nation became a grazing permit.[65]

When no federal agencies really wanted the property it was obtained by the City of Portland to utilize for park and recreational purposes. The city built a sport's car track, drag strip, and sold bonds for a golf course. The race track has been upgraded to accommodate Indianapolis-type cars. Bass and perch were planted in the lakes and sloughs by the Oregon Fish and Game Commission. The golf course, situated close to the railroad fill, was designed by famed golf architect Robert Trent Jones, Jr. Construction contractors received an unexpected bonus when they discovered that the old sewerlines of Vanport City could be utilized for the drainage system. Governor Tom McCall officially opened the course by hitting the first drive at a special press preview on 29 April 1971, and public play started on 1 May. Now that the turf has reached maturity it is capable of hosting a major tournament. Other possibilities, held in abeyance but considered, were a botanical garden, water course, pitch and putt golf course, and play fields (which now exist in what was East Vanport).[66] As long as the disaster had to happen, and in the process destroy the possibility of use for the magnificent college campus it would have made, perhaps it was fortunate that both federal agencies and profit-making enterprises turned away, so that, after the passage of time, in an era of disappearing open space recreation, the land remained for these important uses.

Now, as one again drives over Denver Avenue, grassy, park-like areas intertwined among lagoons and lakes meet the eye. It provides a pleasant prospect, giving the viewer a sense of peace and tranquility that was never present in Vanport City.

IN RETROSPECT

Vanport quickened the tempo of life in Portland and led the city into a new era of change and a new pattern of living, the effects of which still remain strong today. A similar metamorphosis had occurred during the Pacific Coast gold rushes of the mid-nineteenth century. Then young entrepreneurs made Portland into the bustling commercial and transportation center of the Pacific Northwest. In the early twentieth century it lost its place to Seattle and by 1940 had become old and sedate, a quiet city where the wealthy of Oregon went to retire after a successful lifetime of fortune hunting elsewhere. As the war clouds gathered, another entrepreneur selected Portland as the Northwest base of his gigantic shipyard operations, cut through red tape, built Vanport City to house his imported workers, and again pushed Portland into a maelstrom of activity. At the end of the war the shipyards closed, and Vanport was later engulfed by the flood, but Portland never lost the business gains, the quickened pulse, the new city feeling. From all the different impacts of that era, Vanport City remains the most consuming memory.

Vanport left many other legacies. Some were small and relatively unimportant, others larger and of more consequence. There were lessons that could have been learned from the Vanport experience. As usual something was learned, and much was not. The whole notion of Vanport typified the seemingly never-ending mobility of the American people. Vanport Hospital, in spite of its excellent facilities, was too closely connected in the public mind with the idea of government operation of medical facilities, and the medical profession certainly was at least partially responsible for its failure. It was a tiny battle in a war that is still continuing, and although Vanport Hospital was an early casualty, the concept of government assistance in solving medical problems has now been accepted. The flood dealt a damaging blow to the aura of expertise that surrounded the Army Corps of Engineers. Although the memory of the debacle is now almost forgotten, it took two decades to fade away. Perhaps the tragic event had some value in securing an honest reappraisal of the image of infallibility then surrounding science and engineering.

Important, innovative solutions came out of the years at Vanport. Aside from the more mundane architectural planning and construction developments (participated in by the Kaiser Company), there were significant experiments, seldom duplicated again, in large-scale government housing and governmental direction of life patterns. Because all community services had to be provided, Vanport was the most difficult of the new gigantic community housing developments which the federal government hoped would help to win World War II. It proved that when the attitudes of industry, local people, and government coincide, the combination can swiftly and relatively smoothly move the activities of government into new areas. The combined attack on housing, community facilities, and war production had its greatest success in the Vanport experiment. In Richmond, California, on the east side of San Francisco Bay, four big Kaiser yards surrounded the town, and early living conditions were worse than the "Hoovervilles" of the Great Depression. These were eventually replaced by federal government housing which improved the poor conditions but never really solved them.[1] In stark contrast, war production goals at Willow Run largely failed because of opposition of the Ford Motor Company to the establishment of adequate large scale public housing near the plant.[2]

The federal wartime emergency housing program provided the transitional step into a long-range, much expanded permanent housing program. However, this has been confined mainly to high-rise units for the elderly, small projects for low-income families, and scattered rentals of private units. There has been movement towards the Vanport ideal of a large project so located and organized that there would be no stigma attached to living there. Unfortunately, this movement has not proven to be very successful.

In many respects Vanport City came very close to providing an experiment in full socialization of life. The government was responsible for, and rather strictly regulated, the material aspects of living. Vanporters resided in a government building under an extensive list of rules and restrictions. In order to be eligible for this

Its physical remains destroyed, Vanport lived on in the lasting changes it brought to the Portland and Vancouver areas. (OHS neg. 79072).

housing they were required to work at a government approved job. Both parents were encouraged to labor in order to raise productivity, and, because of this, 24-hour day-care of children two to twelve years of age was available. The war boom enabled imported Vanporters to earn high wages in return for this control. As might be expected residents liked the money but not the control, and there was great turnover, although other reasons previously referred to seemed to be responsible for the shifting population.

The government control lessened with the ending of the war and the shipyard closures. However, those who stayed on or moved into Vanport wanted the nursery schools kept going. Even the churches were chagrined when the free heat and custodial services disappeared as a result of weekend closures of public buildings. It was difficult to form any definitive conclusion as to whether the wartime socialization, when weighed in the balance, was responsible for enough discontent to make Vanporters want to forego the advantages. It can be said that the situation was rather calmly accepted by most.

The government child-care centers were closed after the war and the concept abandoned, but it resurfaced in a 1971 bill passed by a Democratic Congress and vetoed by a Republican President, a bill which provided direct funding from the federal to the local level, a near parallel of the Vanport situation.[3]

In addition to the foregoing innovations there were other important Vanport contributions. The introduction and integration of black men and women in sizable numbers into the Portland area must again be mentioned. This proceeded with little incident, and at a time when riots were occurring in Detroit and Harlem (1943). Vanport City, along with other subsidiary agencies of the National Housing Administration, carried an anti-discrimination clause in all its leases and contracts. Previous to World War II, NHA and the Department of the Interior were the only two government agencies to do so.

There were other lessons that could have been learned from Vanport, but were not. The flood caught the community and the surrounding area without a comprehensive disaster plan. Sheriff Pratt acknowledged that this led to mistakes, and after the event he actively tried to promote the formation of such a plan.[4] But as the immediacy of the disaster faded, the American tendency not to worry about the unexpected or unlikely and to cross bridges when you came to them prevailed. The concern of the Vanport Public School administration over the effects of racial imbalance between schools in the city could have been a beacon illuminating the path of what would later become a national problem. The concern went unheeded. Lastly, Vanport and other war centers provided a preview of a new juvenile delinquency, previously unknown in such massive form, and created out of the abdication of parental responsibility. Again, those who saw in it a portent of the future were disregarded,[5] and the comfortable belief that it was a transitory wartime phenomenon remained prevalent.

Vanport encapsuled the America of its time, a time of returning optimism following the depression of the 1930s. There was never a doubt that the war would be won. Vanport City's governors (HAP Board of Commissioners) represented the best of individualistic America, talented, patriotic, seeking no monetary advantage. Although they may have identified their interpretation of capitalism with the public good, they exercised a degree of local control and independence (in spite of federal funding), unknown to the less colorful, more social-minded bureaucrats of today. And after all, Vanport was thought of as temporary and transitory, and the miracle may have been that it worked at all. Yet work it did, in a robust, galvanic manner, full of a buoyant faith in America, a faith in stark contrast to the doubts and hesitations of today. It died as it had lived—quickly and dynamically—but not without its contributions to the future.

Now, as a Portland public park area, nothing of Vanport remains to remind the new generations growing to maturity that Oregon's second largest city was once located there. To those who knew Vanport, it is only on the occasional days when the race cars thunder along what was once Cottonwood Street in the heart of the black district that the real spirit of Vanport City seems to come alive—vibrant, bruising, pulsating.

NOTES

CHAPTER I / The Need, the Idea, the Realization

1. Portland *Oregonian*, (hereafter referred to as *Oregonian*) 26 Sept. 1942.
2. *Oregonian*, 17 Sept. 1942.
3. *Oregonian*, 2 Oct. 1942.
4. *Oregonian*, 28 Sept. 1942.
5. *Oregonian*, 8 Jan. 1943, 24 Dec. 1942.
6. "Vanport City," *Architectural Forum*, 9 (Aug. 1943): 54.
7. *Oregonian*, 20 Sept. 1942.
8. Selden Cowles Menefee, *Assignment: U.S.A.* (New York, 1943), 26.
9. Housing Authority of Portland (hereafter referred to as HAP) File, Scrapbook 1942, *Oregonian*, 26 Sept. 1942.
10. *Oregonian*, 22, 23, 27 Sept. 1942; Menefee, *Assignment: U.S.A.*, 76.
11. Oregon *Journal*, 15 Oct. 1942.
12. *Oregonian*, 17 Sept. 1942.
13. *Oregonian*, 29 Sept. 1942.
14. *Oregonian*, 24 Sept. 1942.
15. *Oregonian*, 25 Sept., 5 Oct. 1942.
16. Menefee, *Assignment: U.S.A.*, 75.
17. *Oregonian*, 20 Sept. 1942, 17 Jan. 1943.
18. *Oregonian*, 13 Aug. 1943.
19. Menefee, *Assignment: U.S.A.*, 77; HAP Vanport File 1942–48, General 10, General Information Folder.
20. HAP Scrapbook 1942, 14 Feb. 1942.
21. HAP Vanport File 1942–48, General 10, Publicity Correspondence Folder; "Vanport City," 2, 53; *Oregonian*, 28 Mar. 1943.
22. HAP University Homes Vanport File, Architects Contract Folder; HAP Vanport File 1942–48, General 10, General Correspondence Folder; HAP File, Scrapbook 1942, *Oregonian*, 9 or 10 Aug. 1942 (specific date not available).
23. "Vanport City," 53, 62.
24. *Oregonian*, 12 Aug. 1943, 22 Sept. 1942; HAP Minutes 1942, 21 Sept.
25. *Oregonian*, 20, 28 Mar. 1943.
26. "The Housing Authority of Portland, Oregon," *Arts and Architecture*, (Sept. 1943), 40; HAP File, Scrapbook 1942, Oregon *Journal*, Sept. 27, 1942; HAP File 1942–48, Management 7, Vanport City Handbook Copy Folder, Construction Report, and General 10, Publicity Correspondence Folder.
27. *Oregonian*, 12 Aug. 1943, 28 Mar. 1943, 17 Sept. 1942, 12 Oct. 1942.
28. HAP File Vanport 1942–48, Management 7, Vanport City Handbook Copy Folder, Construction Report; "Vanport City, Nation's Largest War Housing Project," *Western City*, 19 (Mar. 1943): 29; *Oregonian*, 12 Oct. 1942, 12 Aug. 1943.
29. HAP File Vanport 1942–48, Management 7, Vanport City Handbook Copy Folder, Construction Report; "Vanport City, Nation's Largest War Housing Project," 29; *Oregonian*, 17 Jan. 1943, 12 Oct. 1942.
30. "Vanport City," 54–56.
31. "Vanport City," 56–57; HAP Vanport File 1942–48, General 10, General Correspondence Folder.
32. Editorial, *Oregonian*, 15 Apr. 1946.
33. *Oregonian*, 12 Aug. 1943, 18 Mar. 1943.
34. HAP Minutes, Oct. 1, 1942; *Oregonian*, 18, 23 Sept. 1942.
35. HAP File, Vanport 1942–48, Management 7, Vanport City Handbook Copy Folder, Construction Report; HAP Minutes, Oct. 1, 1942; *Oregonian*, 18, 23 Sept. 1942; Management Correspondence Folder; *Oregonian*, 28 Mar. 1943; HAP University Homes, Vanport File, General 10, Radio Publicity Folder.
36. "Vanport City," 57.

37. HAP File, University Homes and Vanport 1942–48, Landscaping Folder; Oregon *Journal*, 24 June 1943.
38. HAP, *Resident Handbook*, 1; "Vanport City," 55.
39. HAP File, Vanport 1942–48, Management 7, Handbook Copy Folder; HAP File, 1943 Scrapbook, *Oregonian*, 17 May 1943; Oregon *Journal*, 18 May 1943.
40. HAP File, Vanport 1942–48, General 10, Radio Publicity Folder; *Oregonian*, 12, 13 Aug. 1943.
41. *Oregonian*, 12, 13 Aug. 1943.
42. *Oregonian*, 12 Aug. 1943.
43. HAP File, Vanport 1942–48, Management 7, Handbook Copy Folder, Construction Report; HAP Minutes 20 Jan. 1944; Oregon *Journal*, 17 Dec. 1942, *Oregonian*, 12 Aug. 1943.
44. *Oregonian*, 14 Jan. 1943, 28 Mar. 1943; HAP Vanport File 1942–48, Management 7, Tenant Selection Folder; Oregon *Journal*, 15 June 1943, Charlotte Kilbourn and Margaret Lantis, "Elements of Tenant Instability in a War Housing Project," *American Sociological Review*, 11 (Feb. 1946): 58.
45. *Oregonian*, 12 Aug. 1943, 31 May 1948; HAP Vanport File 1942–48, Management 7, Age and Race Folder.
46. HAP Vanport File 1942–48, Management 7, Management Correspondence Folder; Oregon *Journal*, 15 Aug. 1943.
47. HAP Scrapbook 1944, *Oregonian*, 27 Sept., 12 Dec.; HAP Minutes 1944, 17 Aug., 21 Sept., 16 Oct.; Kilbourn and Lantis, "Elements of Tenant Instability in a War Housing Project," 59.
48. HAP Minutes 1945, 4 Jan., 7 June; HAP Scrapbook 1945, *Oregonian*, 4 Feb., 10 Mar.; Oregon *Journal*, 7, 26 Feb.; Portland *Daily Journal of Commerce*, 10 Mar.
49. HAP Vanport File 1942–48, General 10, General Correspondence Folder.
50. HAP Minutes 1945, 17 Aug., 6, 20 Sept., 4 Oct., 1 Nov.; HAP Scrapbook 1945, *Oregonian*, 18 Nov.
51. HAP Management File, All Correspondence, Miscellaneous Folder, July 1946; HAP Minutes 1946, 17 Jan.; HAP Transfer File, Vanport, Aid to Vanport Citizens Folder.

CHAPTER 2 / Life in Vanport

1. Charlotte Kilbourn and Margaret Lantis, "Elements of Tenant Instability in a War Housing Project," *American Sociological Review*, 11 (Feb. 1946): 57–66.
2. HAP Minutes, 4 Apr. 1946.
3. *Oregonian*, 28 Mar. 1943, HAP Scrapbook 1943, Oregon *Journal*, 8 Apr.; HAP Scrapbook 1944, Portland *Daily Journal of Commerce*, 2 Feb.; HAP Minutes 1943, 15 Sept.; HAP Vanport File 1942–48, Management 7, Vanport City Handbook Folder, Construction Report.
4. *Oregonian*, 28 Mar. 1943; Oregon *Journal*, 11 July 1943.
5. *Oregonian*, 4 May 1963.
6. HAP Management File, Vanport City 1942–45, Miscellaneous Folder; Oregon *Journal*, 17 Dec. 1942.
7. HAP, *Resident Handbook*, 2–4; HAP, *Rules and Regulations-Vanport City, Oregon*, (1943); James T. Hamilton, "How Vanport Did a Job," *Progressive Education*, 22 (Mar. 1945): 19; HAP Minutes, 20 Apr. 1944, 2 May 1946; Kilbourn and Lantis, "Elements of Tenant Instability in a War Housing Project," 59.
8. Kilbourn and Lantis, "Elements of Tenant Instability in a War Housing Project," 57.
9. HAP File, Vanport 1942–48, Community Services 11, Tenant Survey Folder.
10. HAP File, Vanport 1942–48, Community Services 11, Tenant Survey Folder.
11. Kilbourn and Lantis, "Elements of Tenant Instability in a War Housing Project," 61–62.
12. Kilbourn and Lantis, "Elements of Tenant Instability in a War Housing Project," 62–66; Menefee, *Assignment: U.S.A.*, 197, 203.
13. Vanport File 1942–48, General 10, General Information Folder; *Business Week*, 745 (11 Dec. 1943): 74; HAP Minutes, 17 Aug. 1944.
14. HAP Vanport File 1942–48, Management 7, Management Correspondence Folder.
15. HAP Management File, Vanport City 1942–45, Complaints Folder; HAP Management File, Project Correspondence 1942–46, Miscellaneous Folder.
16. HAP Management File, General Correspondence 1946; Fire Department 1946 Folder.
17. HAP Vanport File 1942–48, Management 7, Fire Reports, Management Correspondence, Fire Equipment Folders; HAP File, Development All Projects, Construction-Vanport Folder.
18. HAP File, General Administration Prior to 1949, Inter-Office Memos Folder; HAP Scrapbook 1944, Oregon *Journal*, 7 Feb., *Oregonian*, 31 Mar.; HAP Minutes 1944, 6 Apr.; HAP Scrapbook 1945, *Oregonian*, 22 Jan.
19. HAP Minutes 1943, 11 Mar.; HAP File, Vanport 1942–48, Management 7, Fire Department Folder; HAP Scrapbook 1945, Portland *Daily Journal of Commerce*, 18 Dec.
20. HAP File, Vanport 1942–48, Management 7, Tenant Complaints Folder.
21. HAP Management File, Vanport City 1942–45, Complaints Folder; HAP Management File, General Correspondence 1947, Inter-Office Memos Folder; HAP File Vanport 1942–48, Management 7, Management Correspondence Folder.
22. HAP Minutes, 2 Nov. 1944; HAP Scrapbook 1943, Oregon *Journal*, 2 July; Lowell Juilliard Carr and James Edson

Stermer, *Willow Run: A Study of Industrialization and Cultural Inadequacy* (New York, 1952), 119.

23. HAP File, Vanport 1942–48, Management 7, Vanport City Handbook Folder, Construction Report, Fire Reports Folder; Kilbourn and Lantis, "Elements of Tenant Instability in a War Housing Project," 64.

24. HAP Minutes, 18 Aug., 16 Sept., 2 Dec. 1943; 2 Mar. 1944; 7 Feb., 1 Aug., 7 Nov., 5 Dec. 1946; 17 Apr. 1947.

25. Kilbourn and Lantis, "Elements of Tenant Instability in a War Housing Project," 62; HAP File, Management, Vanport City 1942–45, Complaints Folder; HAP Minutes 1944, 4 May.

CHAPTER 3 / Landlord and Big Brother

1. HAP Minutes 1942, 28 Sept., 28 Oct., 5 Nov.; HAP Minutes 1943, 18 Feb.; HAP Transfer File, Vanport Miscellaneous, Lease Folder; *Oregonian*, 6 Nov. 1942.

2. HAP File, General Administration Prior to 1949, Publicity and Photographs Folder.

3. HAP Minutes 1942, 24 Sept.; HAP File, Vanport 1942–48, Management 7, Project Manager Folder; *Oregonian*, 12 Aug. 1943, *Business Week*, 745 (11 Dec. 1943): 74.

4. *Oregonian*, 16 Aug. 1943.

5. Harry Jaeger, Project Manager 1946–48, interview, August, 1971; HAP File, Management, All Projects Correspondence 1942–46, Complaints Folder; HAP Minutes 1945, 1 Nov.

6. Oregon *Journal*, 17 Dec. 1942; HAP, *Rules and Regulations-Vanport City, Oregon*, (1943); HAP, *Resident Handbook*, 1, 4, 7.

7. HAP, *Rules and Regulations-Vanport City, Oregon*, (1943); HAP, *Resident Handbook*, 1–7; HAP Minutes, 1943, 10 May, 2 Dec.

8. HAP, *Rules and Regulations-Vanport City, Oregon*, (1943); HAP, *Resident Handbook*, 1–7; HAP Minutes, 1943, 10 May.

9. HAP, *Rules and Regulations-Vanport City, Oregon*, (1943); HAP, Resident Handbook, 1–7.

10. HAP, *Rules and Regulations-Vanport City, Oregon*, (1943), HAP, Resident Handbook, 1–7.

11. HAP File, Vanport City 1942–48, Management 7, Vanport City Handbook Copy Folder; HAP File, Management, Vanport City 1942–45, Complaints Folder.

12. HAP File, Vanport City 1942–48, General 10, Public Correspondence Folder.

13. HAP File, Vanport City 1942–48, General 10, Public Correspondence Folder.

14. HAP File, Vanport City 1942–48, General 10, Public Correspondence Folder.

15. HAP File, Vanport City 1942–48, General 10, Public Correspondence Folder.

16. *Oregonian*, 12 Aug. 1943, HAP, *From Roses to Rivets*, (1946); Hap File, Vanport 1942–48, Management 7, Handbook Copy Folder.

17. HAP Minutes, 28 Oct. 1942, 16 Sept., 26 Nov., 16 Dec. 1943, 16 Mar., 2 Nov. 1944.

18. HAP File, Vanport 1942–48, Management 7, Project Manager Folder.

19. *Oregonian*, 16 Aug. 1943.

20. *Oregonian*, 16 Aug. 1943.

21. *Oregonian*, 16 Aug. 1943.

22. HAP Minutes 1943, Aug. 18.

23. HAP Minutes 1944, Feb. 17; HAP File, Vanport 1942–48, Management 7, Management Correspondence Folder.

24. HAP File, University Homes and Vanport 1942–48, Landscaping Folder.

25. HAP File, Development All Projects, Construction Vanport Folder, Oregon 35053 Folder.

26. HAP File, Vanport 1942–48, Management 7, Management Correspondence Folder; HAP Minutes, 17 Feb. 1944, 26 Feb. 1946.

27. HAP Minutes, 14 June, 3, 26 Nov. 1943, 1 Nov. 1945, 19 Sept. 1946, 23 Jan. 1947; HAP File, Management, Vanport City 1942–45, Inter-Office Memos Folder.

28. *Oregonian*, 9 Apr. 1943; HAP, *Resident Handbook*, 1; HAP File, Vanport 1942–48, Management 7, Management Correspondence Folder; HAP Minutes, 28 Jan., 17 Feb., 17 Aug. 1944.

29. HAP File, Vanport 1942–48, Management 7, Police Protection and Management Correspondence Folders; HAP, *Resident Handbook*, 4; HAP Minutes, 17 Feb. 1944; Ard M. Pratt, personal letter, 20 Aug. 1971.

30. HAP Minutes, 6 Mar. 1944; Ard M. Pratt, personal letter, 20 Aug. 1971.

31. HAP, *From Roses to Rivets*; HAP, *Resident Handbook*, 3; HAP File, Vanport 1942–48, Management 7, Agreement of Mutual Assistance Folder.

32. HAP File, Vanport 1942–48, Community Services 11, Post Office Folder; Oregon *Journal*, 24 Mar. 1943; HAP, *Resident Handbook*, 2.

33. *Oregonian*, 14 Jan., 28 Mar., 9 Apr. 1943; HAP, *Resident Handbook*, 3, 6.

34. HAP Scrapbook, *Oregonian*, 3 July 1943; HAP File, Vanport 1942–48, Management 7, Vanport City Handbook Copy Folder; HAP File, Management, Vanport City 1942–45, Vanport City Hospital Folder.

35. HAP Minutes, 8 Mar., 10 May, 22 July 1943.

36. HAP Minutes, 6 Oct., 2, 16 Dec. 1943, 6 Jan., 18 May, 1, 9

June, 1944; HAP File, Management, Vanport City, 1942–45, Handbook Copy Folder.

37. HAP File, Management, Vanport City 1942–45, Project Services Folder.

38. HAP File, Management, Vanport City 1942–45, Miscellaneous Folder; HAP File, Vanport 1942–48, Management 7, Fire Reports Folder.

39. HAP File, Vanport 1942–48, General 10, Public Correspondence Folder; HAP File, Management, Vanport City 1942–45, Vanport City Hospital Folder.

40. *Oregonian*, 15 Apr. 1947, HAP Minutes, 24 Oct., 7 Nov. 1946.

41. HAP Minutes, 14, 26 Nov. 1946.

42. HAP Minutes, 5, 19 Dec. 1946; HAP File, Vanport 1942–48, Community Services 11, Northern Permanente Foundation Folder.

43. HAP File, Vanport 1942–48, Community Services 11, Northern Permanente Foundation Folder; HAP Minutes, 15 Apr. 1948.

44. HAP Minutes, 6 May 1948.

45. Eleanor Touhey, "Books for Strangers in a Strange Land, A War Library on the Home Front," *Library Journal*, 69 (15 Jan. 1944): 49–51; HAP File, Vanport 1942–48, Management 7, Vanport City Handbook Copy Folder, Community Services 11, Library Folder.

46. Touhey, "Books for Strangers," 49–51.

47. HAP File, Vanport 1942–48, Community Services 11, Library Folder; HAP File, Vanport City 1942–45, Library Folder.

48. *Oregonian*, 12 Aug. 1943.

49. *Oregonian*, 4 May 1943; HAP File, Vanport 1942–48, General 10, Publicity Correspondence, General Correspondence, General Information Folders; HAP, *From Roses to Rivets*

50. HAP, *From Roses to Rivets*; HAP Scrapbook, *Oregonian*, 8 Jan. 1945; HAP File, Management File, Vanport City 1942–45, Project Services Folder.

51. HAP Files, Management File, Vanport City 1942–45, Project Services Folder; Vanport 1942–48, Community Services 11, Project Services Adviser's Correspondence Folder.

52. HAP File, Vanport 1942–48, Management 7, Vanport City Handbook Copy Folder, Management Correspondence Folder, Community Services 11, Pug Ninomiya Folder; HAP Minutes, 6, 20 Dec. 1945.

53. HAP File, Vanport 1942–48, Community Services 11, Sheriff's Office Folder, General 10, General Correspondence Folder; HAP Minutes, 3 Nov. 1943.

54. HAP File, Vanport 1942–48, Management 7, Handbook Copy Folder.

55. Oregon *Journal*, 15 June 1943; HAP Minutes, 14 June 1943.

56. HAP Minutes, 14, 17 June, 7, 12 July, 4 Aug. 1943.

57. HAP Minutes, 17 Aug., 7 Sept. 1944; HAP Scrapbook, Oregon *Journal*, 19 Oct. 1946; HAP File, Management, General Correspondence 1947, Vanport Newspaper Folder.

58. HAP Minutes, 2, 16 Oct. 1947.

59. HAP File, Management, General Correspondence 1947. Vanport Newspaper Folder.

60. HAP Minutes, 2 Oct. 1947.

61. HAP Minutes, 16 Oct., 6 Nov. 1947; HAP File, Management General Correspondence, Vanport Newspaper Folder.

62. HAP Minutes, 4 Dec. 1947; HAP File, Vanport 1942–48, Community Services 11, Ralph Bennett Folder.

63. HAP File, Vanport 1942–48, Management 7, Management Correspondence Folder; HAP Minutes, 4 Jan. 1945, 17 Jan., 1946.

64. HAP File, Vanport 1942–48, Management 7, Management Correspondence Folder.

65. HAP Minutes, 3 Feb., 2 Mar., 17 Aug. 1944.

66. HAP File, Vanport 1942–48, General 10, Public Correspondence and Radio Publicity Folders; HAP Minutes, 10 May 1943.

67. HAP Minutes, 1 June, 13 July, 5 Oct. 1944.

68. HAP Minutes, 16 Oct. 1944.

69. HAP Minutes, 4 May, 7 Sept., 16, 19 Oct. 1944.

70. HAP Minutes, 19 Oct., 2, 16 Nov. 1944.

71. HAP Minutes, 5 July 1945.

72. HAP Minutes, 2 Nov. 1944, 19 Apr. 1945; *Oregonian*, 20 Nov. 1944; HAP File, Transfer, Vanport, Development of Vanport Industrial Area Folder.

73. *Oregonian*, 14 June 1945.

74. HAP Minutes, 5 July 1945.

75. HAP Minutes, 4 Oct., 1 Nov. 1945, 20 June, 1946; Editorial, *Oregonian*, 15 Apr. 1946.

76. HAP Minutes, 7 June, 5 July 1945.

77. HAP Minutes, 5, 31 July, 2, 17 Aug., 6, 20 Sept., 4, 18 Oct. 1945; HAP File Vanport 1942–48, Management 7, Fire Reports Folder.

78. HAP Minutes, 1 Nov., 6 Dec. 1945; Editorial, *Oregonian*, 15 Apr. 1946; HAP File Management, Vanport City 1942–45, Miscellaneous Correspondence Folder.

79. HAP Minutes, 6, 20 Sept., 18 Oct. 1945.

80. HAP Minutes, 20 Sept., 4 Oct., 1 Nov. 1945.

81. HAP Minutes, 4 Oct. 1945; HAP Scrapbook, Oregon *Journal*, 30 Jan. 1946; Lamar Tooze Sr., former HAP Commissioner, interview, August 1971.

82. HAP Scrapbook, Oregon *Journal*, 30 Jan, 18 Apr. 1946, *Oregonian*, 7 Feb. 1946, Portland *Daily People's World*, 18 Feb. 1946.

83. HAP Minutes, 5 Sept. 1946.
84. HAP File, Vanport City, 1942–45, Adjusted Rents Folder; HAP Minutes, 23 Jan., 6 Feb. 1947.
85. HAP Minutes, 3, 17 Apr., 21 Aug. 1947.
86. HAP Minutes, 4 Mar., 8 Apr. 1948.
87. HAP Minutes, 5 July 1945.
88. HAP Minutes, 8 Mar., 18 Aug. 1943.
89. HAP Minutes, 6 Jan. 1944.
90. HAP Minutes, 6 Feb., 19 June, 24 July, 2 Oct., 6 Nov. 1947; HAP File, Management, Correspondence 1947, Inter-Office Memos Folder.
91. HAP Minutes, 3 Apr. 1947.
92. *Oregonian*, 20 Mar. 1943; HAP Scrapbook, *Oregonian*, 12 Dec. 1945.
93. Charlotte Kilbourn and Margaret Lantis, "Elements of Tenant Instability in a War Housing Project," *American Sociological Review*, 11 (Feb. 1946): 60; HAP File, Vanport 1942–48, General 10 Public Correspondence Folder; Jaeger, private interview; Tooze, interview.
94. HAP Minutes, 10 May, 7, 14 June, 7, 12, 20, July 1943; Oregon *Journal*, 15 June 1943.
95. HAP Minutes, 20 July 1943; HAP File, Vanport 1942–48, Community Services 11, Neighborhood Councils Folder, Management 7, Management Correspondence Folder; HAP File, Management, Vanport City 1942–45, Project Services Folder.
96. HAP Management, Vanport City, 1942–45, Project Services Folder; HAP Minutes, 2 Mar. 1944.
97. HAP Minutes, 4 Apr. 1944, 12 July 1943; James T. Hamilton, "How Vanport Did a Job," *Progressive Education*, 22 (Mar. 1945): 19; HAP Scrapbook, 9 Aug. 1944.
98. Stanley Elkins and Eric McKitrick, "A Meaning for Turner's Frontier I: Democracy in the Old Northwest," *Political Science Quarterly*, 39 (Sept. 1954): 326–29; Stanley Elkins and Eric McKitrick, "II: The Southwest Frontier and New England," 39 (Dec. 1954): .
99. HAP Scrapbook, Oregon *Journal*, 27 May 1946, 10, 26 Mar. 1948, Vanport *Tribune*, 26 Feb. 1948.
100. Oregon *Journal*, 3 Feb. 1946, *Pacific Parade Magazine*, "'Veterans Village' Ready for Occupancy," 1–4.
101. HAP Scrapbooks, Oregon *Journal*, 20 May 1946, 15 June, 13 July, 8 Aug. 1947.
102. HAP Scrapbook, *Oregonian*, 8 Apr. 1945, Oregon *Journal*, 11 Apr. 1945.
103. HAP Scrapbook, *Oregonian*, 8 Apr. 1945, Oregon *Journal*, 28 June 1948.
104. HAP Scrapbook, *Oregonian*, 8 Apr. 1945, *Oregonian*, 3, 9 July 1947; HAP Minutes, 25 July 1947; U.S., Congress, Joint Committee on Housing, *Study and Investigation of Housing, Hearings*, before the Joint Committee on Housing, 80th Cong., 1st sess., Part 4 (Government Printing Office, 1948), 4186–88.

CHAPTER 4 / School

1. HAP Scrapbook, Vanport *Tribune*, 19 Feb. 1948.
2. HAP File, Vanport 1942–48, Management 7, Schools and Gymnasium Folder; James T. Hamilton, "How Vanport Did a Job," *Progressive Education*, 22 (Mar. 1945): 19.
3. HAP Scrapbook, *Oregonian*, 17 Oct. 1942, Oregon *Journal*, 11 Nov. 1942.
4. Hamilton, "How Vanport Did a Job," 17; HAP File, Vanport 1942–48, Community Services 11, Vanport City Schools Folder; HAP Scrapbook, *Oregonian*, 14 May 1944; *Oregonian*, 18 Dec. 1942.
5. "Vanport City," *Architectural Forum*, 9 (Aug. 1943): 58; HAP File, Vanport 1942–48, Management 7, Vanport City Handbook Copy Folder; HAP Scrapbooks, Oregon *Journal*, 30 Apr. 1945, Portland *Daily Journal of Commerce*, 29 June, 2 Aug. 1944; Vanport Public Schools, *Bulletin of General Information*, (1943).
6. HAP Scrapbook, Oregon *Journal*, Mar. 11, 13 July 1943; HAP, *From Roses to Rivets*, (1946); Hamilton, "How Vanport Did a Job," 17–18; Vanport Public Schools, *Bulletin of General Information*, (1944–45).
7. HAP File, Management 1942–45, Columbia District Number 33, 1943 Folder; *Oregonian*, 18 Dec. 1942; HAP Scrapbook, Vanport City, *Tribune*, 19 Feb. 1948.
8. *Oregonian*, 18 Dec. 1942; HAP File, Vanport 1942–48, Community Services 11, Vanport City Schools Folder; HAP Scrapbook, *Oregonian*, 24 Nov. 1942; HAP File, Management 1942–45, Columbia District Number 33, 1943 Folder.
9. HAP File, Management 1942–45, District 33 Folders 1943–45.
10. HAP File, Management 1942–45, District 33 Folders 1943–45.
11. HAP, *Resident Handbook*, 3–4.
12. HAP Scrapbook, *Oregonian*, 24 Nov. 1942; HAP File, Management 1942–45, District 33 Folder, 1943; Hamilton, "How Vanport Did a Job," 19.
13. Hamilton, "How Vanport Did a Job," 18–19; HAP File, Vanport 1942–48, Management 7, Schools and Gymnasium Folder, Vanport City Schools Folder; Vanport Public Schools, *Bulletin of General Information*, (1944–45).

14. Hamilton, "How Vanport Did a Job," 18; *Oregonian*, 8 July 1943.
15. HAP File, Management 1942–45, Columbia District Number 33, 1943 Folder; Vanport Public Schools, *Bulletin of General Information*, (1944–45); *Oregonian*, 22 June 1943.
16. HAP File, Vanport 1942–48, Management 7, Tenant Handbook; Vanport Public Schools, *Bulletin of General Information*, (1944–45).
17. HAP File, Management, General Correspondence 1947, Inter-Office Memos Folder; HAP File, Vanport 1942–48, Community Services 11, Vanport City Schools Folder; HAP Minutes, 17 Jan. 1946.
18. HAP File, Vanport 1942–48, Management 7, Repairs to School Buildings Damaged by Fire Folder; HAP File, Management, Vanport City 1942–45, Project Services Folder.
19. HAP File, Vanport 1942–48, Community Services 11, Vanport City Schools Folder; HAP Minutes, 1 Aug. 1946.
20. HAP File, Vanport 1942–48, Community Services 11, Vanport City Schools Folder; *Oregonian*, 10 Mar. 1946.
21. HAP Minutes, 19 Apr. 1945, 7 Nov. 1946.
22. HAP Minutes, 5 Dec. 1946, 23 Jan., 20 Feb., 19 June 1947; HAP File, Vanport 1942–48, Community Services 11, Vanport City Schools Folder.
23. HAP Minutes, 5 Dec. 1946, 23 Jan., 20 Feb., 19 June 1947; HAP File, Vanport 1942–48, Community Services 11, Vanport City Schools Folder.
24. HAP Minutes, 23 Jan. 1947; HAP Scrapbooks, *Oregonian*, 19 Sept. 1947, 13 Jan. 1948, 7 Mar. 1948, Oregon *Journal*, 17 Oct. 1947; HAP File Vanport 1942–48, Community Services 11, Vanport City Schools Folder.
25. HAP Scrapbook, Oregon *Journal*, 9 Sept. 1947
26. HAP Scrapbook, *Oregonian*, 27 Aug. 1947.
27. HAP Scrapbook, *Oregonian*, 27, 29 Aug., 8 Sept. 1947
28. HAP Minutes, 4 Sept., 16 Oct. 1947; HAP Scrapbook, *Oregonian*, 9 Sept. 1947, Oregon *Journal*, 9 Sept. 1947, HAP File, Vanport 1942–48, Community Services 11, Vanport City Schools Folder.
29. HAP Scrapbook, 5 Sept. 1947.
30. HAP File, Vanport 1942–48, Community Services 11, Vanport City Schools Folder.
31. HAP Minutes, 16 Oct. 1947; HAP File, Vanport 1942–48, Community Services 11, Vanport City Schools Folder.
32. HAP Minutes, 16 Oct. 1947; HAP File, Vanport 1942–48, Community Services 11, Vanport City Schools Folder.
33. HAP File, Vanport 1942–48, Community Services 11, Vanport City Schools Folder; HAP Scrapbook, *Oregonian*, 27 Nov. 1947.
34. HAP Minutes, 16 Oct. 1947.
35. HAP Scrapbook, Vanport *Tribune*, 26 Feb. 1948, *Oregonian*, 20, 25 Feb. 1948.
36. HAP Minutes, 19 Feb., 1 Apr., 6 May 1948; HAP Scrapbook, *Oregonian*, 20 Jan., 12 May 1948; HAP File, Vanport 1942–48, Community Services 11, Vanport City Schools Folder.
37. HAP Scrapbook, *Oregonian*, 22 Dec. 1946.
38. HAP Scrapbook, *Oregonian*, 22 Dec. 1946; Stephen Epler, *First Annual Report of the Vanport Extension Center of the General Extension Division of the Oregon State System of Higher Education* (Vanport City 1946–47); Don R. Hammitt, "Oregon Solves College Overcrowding," *National Education Association Journal*, 35 (Oct. 1946): 389.
39. HAP File, Vanport 1942–48, Community Services 11, Vanport Extension Center Folder; HAP Minutes, 21 Feb. 1946.
40. HAP Scrapbook, *Oregonian*, 21 Feb. 1946; HAP Minutes, 21 Feb. 1946; HAP File, Vanport 1942–48, Community Services 11, Vanport Extension Center Folder.
41. "The Vanport Idea," *Time*, 48 (29 July 1946): 51; HAP Scrapbook, *Oregonian*, 22 Dec. 1946.
42. HAP Scrapbook, *Oregonian*, 11 June 1946; Oregon State System of Higher Education, Leaflet Series, no. 325 (Eugene, Ore. 1 Apr. 1946).
43. HAP Scrapbook, *Oregonian*, 19 June 1946; Epler, *First Annual Report of the Vanport Extension Center*; HAP File, Vanport 1942–48, Community Services 11, Vanport Extension Center Folder.
44. HAP File, Vanport 1942–48, Community Services 11, Vanport Extension Center Folder; HAP File, Management, All Projects Correspondence 1942–46, Miscellaneous Folder; HAP Minutes, 19 Sept 1946.
45. HAP Minutes, 1 Aug. 1946.
46. HAP Scrapbook, *Oregonian*, 30 Aug. 1946.
47. HAP Scrapbook, *Oregonian*, 30 Aug. 1946. *Oregonian* and Oregon *Journal*, 30 Aug. 1946.
48. HAP Scrapbook, *Oregonian*, 30 Aug. 1946, Oregon *Journal*, 27 Sept., 17 Oct. 1946; HAP File, Community Services 11, 16 Oct. 1946, Vanport Extension Center Folder.
49. Epler, *First Annual Report of the Vanport Extension Center*, 2, 10, 14,; HAP File, Vanport 1942–48, Community Services 11, Vanport Extension Center Folder; Jean Phyllis Black, "Vanport Starts Them to College," *Library Journal*, 72 (1 Dec. 1947): 1648.
50. Epler, *First Annual Report of the Vanport Extension Center*, 8; Black, "Vanport Starts Them to College," 1646–48.
51. HAP File, Vanport 1942–48, Community Services 11, Vanport Extension Center Folder; Epler, *First Annual Report of the Vanport Extension Center*, 5; HAP Scrapbook, *Oregonian*, 22 Dec. 1946.

52. HAP Minutes, 20 Feb. 1947; HAP File, Vanport 1942–48, Community Services 11, Vanport Extension Center Folder, Vanport City Schools Folder.
53. HAP File, Management, General Correspondence 1947, Vanport Extension Center Folder for 1947.
54. Epler, *First Annual Report of the Vanport Extension Center*, 3–4; Stephen E. Epler, "Do Veterans Make Better Grades Than Non-Veterans," *School and Society*, 66 (4 Oct. 1947): 270; Oregon State System of Higher Education, Leaflet Series, no. 349 (Eugene, Ore. 1 Apr. 1947); HAP File, Vanport 1942–48, Community Services 11, Vanport Extension Center Folder, Vanport College Quiz.
55. *Oregonian*, 26, 27 May 1947; HAP File, Vanport 1942–48, Community Services 11, Vanport Extension Center Folder.
56. Epler, *First Annual Report of the Vanport Extension Center*, 2, 11, 12.
57. U.S., Congress, Joint Committee on Housing, *Study and Investigation of Housing, Hearings*, before the Joint Committee on Housing, 80th Cong., 1st sess., Part 4 (Government Printing Office, 1948), 4186–88; HAP Minutes, 19 June, 24 July 1947; HAP File, Vanport 1942–48, Communnity Services 11, Vanport Extension Center Folder.
58. HAP File, Vanport 1942–48, Community Services 11, Vanport Extension Center Folder; Black, "Vanport Starts Them to College," 1648; HAP Minutes, 20 May 1948.
59. HAP Scrapbook, Oregon *Journal*, 26 Mar. 1948, *Oregonian*, 17 May 1948; HAP Minutes, 15 Apr. 1948.

CHAPTER 5 / Crime and Delinquency

1. Lowell Juilliard Carr and James Edson Stermer, *Willow Run: A Study of Industrialization and Cultural Inadequacy* (New York, 1952); Robert J. Havighurst and H. Gerthon Morgan, *The Social History of a War Boom Community* (New York, 1951).
2. "Day Nursery in the Tree Shaded Park," Painting for the Portland General Electric Company.
3. HAP File, Management, Vanport City 1942 1945, Miscellaneous and Project Services Folders; HAP File, Vanport 1942–48, Community Services 11, Project Services Adviser's Correspondence Folder; HAP Minutes, 11 July, 1 Aug. 1946.
4. HAP Minutes, 7, 21 Feb. 1946, 18 Mar. 1948.
5. HAP File, Management, Vanport City 1942–45, District 33 Folder; Selden Cowles Menefee, *Assignment: U.S.A.* (New York, 1943), 232.
6. HAP Minutes, 17 Aug. 1944; HAP File, Management, Vanport City 1942–45, Project Services Folder.
7. HAP File, Management, Vanport City 1942–45, Project Services Folder.
8. HAP File, Management, Vanport City 1942–45, Project Services Folder.
9. HAP File, Management, Vanport City 1942–45, Project Services Folder.
10. HAP Scrapbook, Oregon *Journal*, Nov. 19, 1944.
11. HAP Scrapbook, Oregon *Journal*, Nov. 19, 1944.
12. HAP File, Management, Vanport City 1942–45, Miscellaneous Folder; HAP Minutes, 15 Mar. 1945, 20 Mar. 1947.
13. HAP Minutes, 17 Jan. 1946, 20 Mar., 5 June 1947.
14. HAP File, Vanport 1942–48, Management 7, Police Protection Folder; Ard M. Pratt Sr., personal letter, 20 Aug. 1971.
15. HAP Minutes, 7 July 1943, 5 Apr. 1945; HAP File, Vanport 1942–48, Community Services 11, Commercial Leases Folder.
16. HAP Minutes, 18 May 1944; HAP File, Vanport 1942–1948, Management 7, Management Correspondence Folder.
17. HAP Minutes, 17 Aug. 1945.
18. HAP File, Vanport 1942–48, Management 7, Police Protection Folder.
19. HAP File, Vanport 1942–48, Management 7, Police Protection Folder.
20. HAP Minutes, 20 Feb., 6 Mar. 1947.

CHAPTER 6 / Race

1. HAP Minutes, 18 Oct. 1945.
2. *Oregonian*, 4 Oct. 1942; HAP Minutes, 17 Jan. 1946.
3. HAP File, Vanport 1942–48, General 10, General Correspondence and Public Correspondence Folders; HAP File, General Administration Prior to 1949, Racial Relations Folder.
4. HAP Minutes, 18 Oct. 1945; HAP File, General Administration Prior to 1949, Racial Relations Folder.
5. HAP Scrapbook, *Oregonian*, 9 Oct. 1943; HAP Minutes, 4, 18 May 1944; HAP File, Vanport 1942–48, General 10, General Correspondence Folder.
6. HAP Scrapbook, *Oregonian*, Editorial, 18 Dec. 1944.
7. HAP Minutes, 21 June 1945; HAP File, Vanport 1942–48, Community Services 11, Project Services Adviser's Correspondence Folder.
8. HAP Minutes, 20 July, 3 Aug. 1944; Charlotte Kilbourn and Margaret Lantis, "Elements of Tenant Instability in a War Housing Project," *American Sociological Review*, 11 (Feb. 1946): 57–66.
9. HAP Minutes, 16 Sept. 1943; Ard M. Pratt Sr., personal letter, 20 Aug. 1971.

10. HAP File, Vanport 1942–48, Management 7, Police Protection Folder.
11. HAP File, Vanport 1942–48, Management 7, Police Protection Folder.
12. HAP Minutes, 16 Sept. 1943.
13. HAP Minutes, 16 Sept. 1943; 1 Aug., 17 Oct. 1946; 18 Mar., 15 Apr., 20 May 1948.
14. HAP Minutes, 18 Mar. 1948; Pratt, personal letter.
15. HAP Scrapbook, *Oregonian*, 24 June 1945; HAP Management File, Vanport City 1942–45, Miscellaneous Folder.
16. HAP Scrapbook, Oregon *Journal*, 10 July 1945.
17. HAP Minutes, 17 Jan. 1946.
18. HAP File, Management Vanport City 1942–45, Community Activities Folder.
19. HAP File, Vanport 1942–48, Management 7, Police Protection Folder; Kilbourn and Lantis, "Elements of Tenant Instability in a War Housing Project," 61; HAP File, Vanport 1942–45, Community Activities and Complaint Folders.
20. HAP Minutes, 12 July, 4, 18 Aug. 1943.
21. HAP File, General Administration Prior to 1949, Racial Relations Folder.
22. HAP File, General Administration Prior to 1949, Racial Relations Folder.
23. Kilbourn and Lantis, "Elements of Tenant Instability in a War Housing Project," 61; HAP File, Management Vanport City 1942–45, Project Services Folder.
24. HAP File, Management Vanport City 1942–45, Project Services Folder; HAP File, Vanport 1942–48, Community Services 11, Project Services Adviser's Correspondence Folder.
25. HAP File, Management, Vanport City 1942–45, Project Services Folder; HAP File, Vanport 1942–48, Management 7, Vanport Residents, Age and Race Folder.
26. HAP File, Vanport 1942–48, Management 7, Management Correspondence Folder.
27. HAP File, Management, Vanport City 1942–45, Complaints Folder.
28. HAP File, General Administration Prior to 1949, Racial Relations Folder.
29. HAP Minutes, 5 July 1945, 7 Mar. 1946.
30. HAP Scrapbook, Portland *Northwest Clarion*, 4 Oct. 1946.
31. HAP Minutes, 17 Oct. 1946; HAP File, Vanport 1942–48, Community Services 11, Vanport Extension Center Folder.
32. HAP Minutes, 5, 25 June 1947.
33. *Keesing's Research Report, Race Relations in the U.S.A. 1954–68* (New York, 1970), 238.
34. HAP Scrapbook, *Oregonian*, 6 Jan. 1948.
35. HAP Minutes, 8 Jan., 18 Mar. 1948; HAP Scrapbook, *Oregonian*, 9 Jan., 6, 21 Feb. 1948.

CHAPTER 7 / The Image

1. Eleanor Touhey, "Books for Strangers in a Strange Land, A War Library on the Home Front," *Library Journal*, 69 (15 Jan. 1944): 49–52; *Business Week*, no. 719 (12 June 1943): 18; "The Housing Authority of Portland, Oregon," *Arts and Architecture*, 48 (Sept. 1943): 39–43; HAP Scrapbook, Portland *Daily Journal of Commerce*, 16 June 1943.
2. "Vanport City, Nation's Largest War Housing Project," *Western City*, 19 (March 1943): 30; HAP Scrapbook, Oregon *Journal*, 24 June 1943; "Vanport City, U.S.A.," Portland *Bo's'n's Whistle*, 20 May 1943, 8; HAP Scrapbook, *Oregonian*, 21 Oct. 1943; Oregon *Journal*, 15 Aug. 1943.
3. "Vanport City," *Architectural Forum*, 9 (Aug. 1943): 1, 60.
4. HAP File containing 1943 Scrapbooks.
5. HAP Scrapbook, *Oregonian* and Oregon *Journal*, 21 Nov. 1943; HAP File, Vanport 1942–48, General 10, Public Correspondence Folder.
6. HAP File, Vanport 1942–48, General 10, Public Correspondence Folder.
7. HAP File, Vanport 1942–48, General 10, Public Correspondence Folder; HAP Scrapbook, Oregon *Journal*, 6 Aug. 1943.
8. HAP Scrapbook, Portland *Daily Journal of Commerce*, 18 Mar., 3 May 1944, *Oregonian*, 25 June 1944, Oregon *Journal*, 25 June 1944; HAP Minutes, 17 Mar. 1944.
9. HAP Minutes, 3 Aug. 1944, 1 Feb., 19 Apr. 1945.
10. The film, "A College Comes To Housing," (ten minutes) referred to in chapter 3 contains all there is as far as the writer knows.
11. HAP, *From Roses to Rivets*, (1946).
12. James T. Hamilton, "How Vanport Did a Job," *Progressive Education*, 22 (Mar. 1945): 19; HAP Minutes, 5, 18 July, 6 Sept., 20 Dec. 1945.
13. HAP File, General Correspondence 1947, Inter-Office Memorandum 1946; HAP File, Management Vanport City 1942–45, Miscellaneous Folder.
14. HAP Scrapbook, *Oregonian*, 11, 14 Jan. 1946, Oregon *Journal*, 14, 15, 17, 21 Jan. 1946.
15. HAP Minutes, 7 Feb. 1946.
16. HAP Minutes, 2, 16 May, 11 July 1946.
17. HAP File, Vanport City, 1942–48, Community Services 11, Vanport City Schools Folder; HAP Minutes, 2 May, 24 Oct., 14 Nov. 1946; HAP Scrapbook, *Oregonian*, 12 Dec. 1945.
18. HAP Management File, All Project Correspondence 1942–46, Miscellaneous Folder.
19. HAP Minutes, 16 Oct., 6 Nov. 1947, 4 Mar. 1948.
20. "Oregon: Day of Tragedy," *Newsweek*, 31 (7 June 1948): 24; Phiz Mezey, "The Real Vanport Disaster: Housing," *New Republic* (5 July 1948), 7.

CHAPTER 8 / Oblivion

1. "Vanport City, U.S.A.," Portland *Bo's'n's Whistle*, 20 May 1943, 8.
2. *Oregonian*, Apr. 2, 1948; HAP Minutes, Sept. 16, 1948; HAP Transfer File, Vanport Last Aid to Vanport Citizens Folder; HAP Scrapbook, *Oregonian*, 2 June 1948.
3. *Oregonian*, 31 May 1948, 1 June 1948.
4. HAP Minutes, 20 May 1948; Harry D. Freeman, Harry D. Jaeger, and Roy W. Taylor, "Housing Authority of Portland Report on Vanport City Flood Disaster," 1 June 1948, 4 (Manuscript Collection MSS 392, Oregon Historical Society [OHS], Portland); Martin T. Pratt Papers (Manuscript Collection MSS 698 Vanport Flood, OHS, Portland).
5. Freeman, Jaeger, and Taylor, "Report on Flood Disaster," 1.
6. Freeman, Jaeger, and Taylor, "Report on Flood Disaster," 2; Pratt Papers.
7. HAP Transfer File, Vanport Last, Vanport Folder (Index of Vanport Records); HAP Minutes, Special Meeting 2 Nov. 1948.
8. *Oregonian*, 31 May 1943; Lois and Fred Johnson, "Some Through the Flood," (mimeographed booklet privately produced), 5, 8; *Oregonian*, 26 May 1968; Freeman, Jaeger, and Taylor, "Report on Flood Disaster," 3.
9. Freeman, Jaeger, and Taylor, "Report on Flood Disaster," 2, 3; HAP Minutes, Special Meeting, 2 Nov. 1948.
10. Freeman, Jaeger, and Taylor, "Report on Flood Disaster," 2, 3.
11. *Oregonian*, 31 May 1948; 26 May 1968.
12. Roy O. Edwards, "Vanport City—'Born in War Died in Flood,'" *Journal of Housing*, 5 (June 1948): 147; Pratt Papers.
13. *Oregonian*, May 31, 1948; Stephen E. Epler, "College Lost in Flood to Continue," *School and Society*, 68 (24 July 1948): 54.
14. Pratt Papers; *Oregonian*, 31 May 1948.
15. *Oregonian*, 31 May 1948.
16. *Oregonian*, 31 May 1948; *Oregonian*, 27 June 1948.
17. Pratt Papers; *Oregonian*, 31 May 1948.
18. Pratt Papers; *Oregonian*, 31 May 1948.
19. Pratt Papers; *Oregonian*, 31 May 1948.
20. *Oregonian*, 1 June 1948.
21. *Oregonian*, 1 June 1948; Pratt Papers.
22. *Oregonian*, 31 May 1948.
23. *Oregonian*, 31 May 1948.
24. *Oregonian*, 31 May 1948; *Oregonian*, 1 June 1948; 26 May 1968.
25. *Oregonian*, 31 May 1948.
26. *Oregonian*, 31 May 1948; 1 June 1948.
27. Pratt Papers; *Oregonian*, 2 June 1948.
28. HAP Minutes, Special Meeting 1 June 1948; *Oregonian*, 3 June 1948.
29. HAP Minutes, Special Meetings 1, 11 June, Regular Meeting June 17, 28, July 1, 1948; Edwards, "Vanport City," 147.
30. Pratt Papers.
31. Pratt Papers; "Oregon: Day of Tragedy," *Newsweek*, 31 (7 June 1948): 24; HAP Transfer File, Vanport Last, Aid to Vanport Citizens Folder; *Oregonian*, 2 June 1948.
32. Pratt Papers; Stewart Holbrook, "The Mythmakers," *New Yorker*, 24 (31 July 1948), 35–36; *Oregonian*, 3 June 1948.
33. Pratt Papers; *Oregonian*, 31 May 1948; 26 May 1968; Richard L. Neuberger, "One of Our Cities Is Missing," *The Nation*, 166, (12 June 1948), 652.
34. *Oregonian*, 2 June 1948; 26 May 1968; Pratt Papers; HAP Scrapbook, *Oregonian*, 10 Sept. 1948; HAP Transfer File, Vanport Miscellaneous, Vanport Casualty List Folder.
35. Johnson, "Some Through the Flood," 4–12.
36. *Oregonian*, 31 May 1948.
37. *Oregonian*, 31 May 1948.
38. Pratt Papers.
39. Freeman, Jaeger, and Taylor, "Report on Flood Disaster," 4–5, copy with written notations inserted in HAP Transfer File, Vanport Last, Index of Vanport Records (for hearing) Folder.
40. Freeman, Jaeger, and Taylor, "Report on Flood Disaster," 4–5, copy with written notations inserted in HAP Transfer File, Vanport Last, Index of Vanport Records (for hearing) Folder.
41. *Oregonian*, 1 June 1948.
42. *Oregonian*, 27 June 1948.
43. *Oregonian*, 1 June 1948.
44. *Oregonian*, 31 May 1948, 1 June 1948.
45. *Oregonian*, 31 May 1948, 1 June 1948.
46. *Oregonian*, 1 June 1948.
47. *Oregonian*, 1 June 1948.
48. Phiz Mezey, "The Real Vanport Disaster: Housing," *New Republic*, 119 (5 July 1948): 7; HAP Scrapbook, 1949, *Oregonian*, 3 Jan., 21 July, Oregon *Journal*, 3, 8 Jan.; Neuberger, "One of Our Cities Is Missing," 652; *Oregonian*, 19 June 1948; Pratt Papers.
49. *Oregonian*, 31 May 1948; Pratt Papers.
50. HAP Minutes, 28 June, 1 July 1948; *Oregonian*, 19 June 1948; Pratt Papers.
51. HAP Scrapbook, Oregon *Journal*, 21, 30 July, 21 Aug. 1948.
52. HAP Minutes, 19 Aug., 16 Dec. 1948, 7 April, 20 Dec. 1949; HAP File, Vanport 1942–48, Community Services 11, Vanport Extension Center Folder; "Housing: Vanport Flood Sale," *Newsweek*, 33 (31 Jan. 1949): 60.
53. *Oregonian*, 1 May 1949.
54. *Oregonian*, 1 June 1948.
55. HAP Minutes, 28 June, 21 Oct. 1948.
56. HAP Minutes, 2 Nov., 16 Dec. 1948.

57. HAP Minutes, Mar. 17, 1949.
58. HAP File, Two Old Scrapbooks, *Oregonian*, 7, 10 Aug. 1951, Oregon *Journal*, 9 Aug. 1951.
59. HAP File, Two Old Scrapbooks, Oregon *Journal*, 10, 13 Aug. 1951, *Oregonian*, 15 Aug. 1951.
60. HAP Minutes, 2 Nov. 1948.
61. HAP Minutes, 29 Sept. 1948.
62. HAP File, Two Old Scrapbooks, Oregon *Journal*, 9 Aug. 1951.
63. HAP File, Vanport 1942–48, Management 7.
64. *Oregonian*, 26 May 1968, 4M, 5 May 1972.
65. HAP Minutes, 18 Mar. 1948, 29 Sept. 1949; HAP File, Vanport 1942–48, Community Services 11, Vanport City schools Folder; HAP Scrapbook, Portland *Daily Journal of Commerce*, 4 Jan 1949; HAP File, Vanport Miscellaneous, Edwin A. Meng Lease Folder.
66. *Oregonian*, 26 May 1968, 30 Apr. 1971; Vancouver, Wash. *Columbian*, 16 Apr. 1971, 18, 4 May 1971, 17.

CHAPTER 9 / In Retrospect

1. Selden Cowles Menefee, *Assignment: U.S.A.* (New York, 1943), 73–74.
2. Selden Cowles Menefee, *Assignment: U.S.A.* (New York, 1943), 109, 153.
3. Vancouver, Wash. *Columbian*, Editorial, 13 Dec. 1971, 16.
4. Martin. T. Pratt Papers (Manuscript Collection MSS 698 Vanport Flood, Oregon Historical Society, Portland).
5. Menefee, *Assignment: U.S.A.*, 232.

INDEX

150

COLOPHON

Vanport is set in Mergenthaler Times Roman, a photo-composition typeface based on the hot-metal face originally commissioned in 1931 by *The Times* of London for its newspapers. The design was supervised by Stanley Morison for the Monotype Corporation. The display type is Linotype Alternate Gothic No. 2 Bold, a hot-metal face that enjoyed great popularity during the thirties and forties.

Vanport is printed on 80 lb. Shasta Suede with white 100 lb. Shasta Suede for endsheets. The cover is 10 pt. Carolina Coated stock, printed in PMS 199 (red) and PMS 280 (blue) inks.

The production of *Vanport* was accomplished through the cooperation and professional skill of the following:
TYPESETTING: G & S Typesetters, Inc., Austin, Texas
Chapel Printing Service, Inc., Portland, Oregon (display)
PRINTING: Print Tek West, Salem, Oregon
BINDING: Lincoln and Allen, Portland, Oregon
PAPER: The Unisource Corporation, Portland, Oregon
MAPS: John Tomlinson, Portland, Oregon

Produced and designed by
the Oregon Historical Society Press.